More Things to Do with Toddlers and Twos

Written and illustrated by

KAREN MILLER

TelShare Publishing, Inc.

Sixth Printing, January 1999

International Standard Book Number 0-910287-08-2

Library of Congress Catalog Card Number 90-70984

Written and Illustrated by Karen Miller

Dedication

This book is dedicated to Lisa Haley Ogden, my granddaughter, who has just launched herself into the exciting adventure of toddlerhood. May you and your parents have a wonderful time!

Table of Contents

Introduction

All toddlers and two-year-olds deserve loving, consistent care. They have a right to greet the world eagerly and with confidence. They need a safe and healthy place to grow where they can learn social and intellectual skills—a place where they can receive pleasure from the ideas of others, and where their own ideas are valued. Most of all, they deserve a place where they can PLAY because it is through play that children learn and develop a sense of who they are.

My goal in writing this book is to offer encouragement, help and abiding respect for friends and admirers of toddlers—you who are privileged to work with this age group. Whether you are a caregiver of children in a center-based setting, a family child care provider or a parent wanting to have more fun with your own child, this book is written for you.

Since writing *Things to Do with Toddlers and Twos*, I have had the opportunity to speak to, and learn from, many groups of people around the country who work with this challenging and wonderful age group. Many fine teachers/caregivers have shared their enthusiasms and ideas. Often someone would say to me, "You know that idea in your book . . . well, I've added a new twist. Here's what I do," or, "Here's something I've enjoyed doing with my little ones that didn't appear in your book . . ." It's not often that a writer has the chance to say, "Oh . . . and one more thing . . ." I'm glad that I can have this opportunity to spread around more good ideas.

In writing a "sequel," an author can never be certain that the reader has read the first book. Rather than repeating much material, after major topic sections, I have indicated where to look for related activities in *Things to Do with Toddlers and Twos* (TelShare Publishing Co. Inc., Chelsea, MA, 1984). Although this book is meant to stand on its own, it is *also* meant to be a companion to the first book.

To organize the material in this book, I used as a guide the thirteen "Functional Areas" of the Child Development Associate (CDA) credentialing program. I find that these topic areas: safety, health, the learning environment, physical development (fine-motor and gross motor), cognitive development (becoming active thinkers and dramatic play), communication (language development and music), creative development (sensory activities and art), sense of self, social development, guidance and discipline, working with families, program management (curriculum development and routines) and professionalism "cover the bases" well and provide a good framework for someone investigating the field of early childhood education.

The only problem is that many activities could fall under several of these headings. Stacking blocks, for instance, could be considered a creative activity as well as a physical—fine motor activity. So, for the convenience of people who are working toward a CDA credential, after each activity I have listed in parentheses other related functional areas.

The only CDA Functional Area I chose not to cover in this book is that of health. This topic is so important, and the information so specific that it is beyond the scope of this book to do it justice. Instead, I urge the reader to read *Healthy Young Children, A Manual for Programs*, edited by Abby Shapiro Kendrick, Roxanne Kaufmann and Katherine P. Messenger, and published NAEYC, Washington, DC, 1988. This, in my opinion, is *the* definitive book on health and safety in child care settings. It is extremely well-researched and reflects the most current thinking. There is much useful information in an easy to use format.

(I should add that I have no association with CDA myself, other than respecting the program and being supportive of it. To find out more about CDA, contact: The Council for Early Childhood Professional Recognition, 1718 Connecticut Ave. N.W., Washington, D.C. 20009; 800-424-4310.)

Successful teaching of any age group requires more than a collection of activities to do with children. You need an understanding of how these young children learn, what they need from you for their emotional and social growth. You also need some good strategies and organizational skills to get things done. I have tried to weave all of these things together. The ideas presented in this book come from real people who are actually working with toddlers and two year olds, things I have personally observed. I feel privileged to be able to act as a "networking agent" for them. I would like to give special thanks to Dr. Katie Best Butler, Cynthia Hunt, Melode Hurst, Barb Lust, Patty Ohl, and Kalen Saxton for sharing their very special insights.

People who work with toddlers and two-year-olds successfully are very special. Some say that they have the quality of patience, but that is not the right word. Patience implies something negative that must be tolerated. Flexibility is a better word. A teacher of toddlers and twos needs both physical and mental flexibility . . . and spontaneity . . . and joy. One reason we read books is to get new ideas and expand our understandings. Another reason is to get re-confirmed in what we believe. If you are just starting out, I hope the ideas in this book are helpful. If you are an "old master" at working with toddlers, I hope this book offers you reinforcement. Carry on with enthusiasm!

CHAPTER 1

A Place for Living and Growing

Your toddlers are "living" a large portion of their lives in the space you set up for them. The environment should be attractive and comfortable for children and adults alike and allow a wide range of physical activity. How you divide, organize and equip your space indoors and outdoors, has a great influence on the effectiveness of your program.

In designing an environment for toddlers and two-year-olds, think about the nature of this age group—their compulsive activities. They are climbers; they love to crawl into small spaces. Try to plan your environment so that there are many legitimate ways children can practice these activities. They also love to dump containers full of toys and carry objects all over the room, so organize the environment well to simplify clean-up.

BASIC INDOOR INTEREST CENTERS

It works well to divide your space into "interest centers" according to major learning functions. As well as keeping your room attractive and organized, interest centers help the adult plan. Remembering the importance of the "novelty factor" in capturing children's interest, you can consciously change something in each interest center each week. Possible interest centers might include, art; blocks; books and language; dramatic play (housekeeping); fine motor (manipulatives); gross motor; science; and sensory play. What follows is a description of some basic equipment and organization tips. There are many other fine pieces of equipment available, and don't be afraid to improvise and make your own things, keeping safety in mind. Do not limit yourself to these interest centers,

1

and do not feel you necessarily must have all of them all the time. Your room should reflect your own interests and the interests of your children.

Art Center

Equipment:

> *Low easel*
> *Plastic smocks*
> *Table*
> *Various art supplies*

Your art area should be over hard flooring near the sink for easier clean-up. The tables you use for eating could double as your art tables. Do art projects with only 3 or 4 children at a time, or individually, never with a large group. Smocks can be hung on a mug rack on the wall near-by. You need not leave art materials out and accessible to impulsive toddlers as you would with older children. Rather, bring materials out for planned projects and put them away in an adult storage closet when you are through. With older two-year-olds you can begin to leave certain materials such as paper and crayons available to them at free-choice time.

Block Center

Equipment:

1 or 2 shelves
Plastic or rubber animals
Small people
Toy vehicles
*Wooden unit blocks**

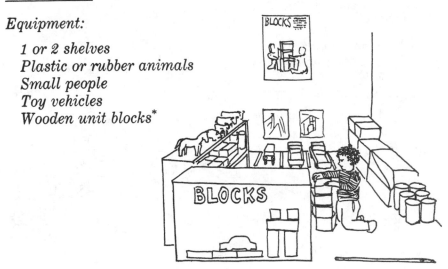

At least one of the following: large cardboard blocks; large,
vinyl-coated nylon covered foam blocks; large plastic blocks;
homemade milk carton or diaper box blocks; large "waffle"
blocks

Store blocks on a shelf, or outline shapes directly on the floor
with tape for large blocks. If you have wooden unit blocks, make
colored contact paper shapes that correspond to the various shapes
and put them on the shelf where the blocks are stored. Place pictures
of other toys directly on the shelf, where each toy should be put
away. You could use tape to make "parking places" on the floor
for toy vehicles. Place your shelf or shelves in the middle of the
room, facing the wall or corner to divide off the area, rather than
against the wall facing out. This helps contain the blocks to one
portion of the room. You might also put a tape boundary on the
floor.

---

* Wooden unit blocks are recommended for older two-year-olds rather than young
toddlers. Provide several basic shapes—single and double rectangle units,
squares, triangles, and a few cylinders. Start with just one shape and add others,
increasing the number of blocks as the year progresses.

Books and Language

Equipment:

*A selection of good picture
    books and homemade
    books
Stable bookshelf
Soft, cozy items like large
    pillows
Stuffed animals to read to*

*Develop your book area into a warm, comfortable and inviting
place. Making the area cozy gives the message that books are a
"comfort item," and that reading is a pleasant, relaxing thing to
do. Be sure to reinforce this by ending up in that spot yourself
as often as you can in free moments of the day. There should be
good lighting, and it should be located in a relatively quiet place,
away from blocks and gross motor toys. Display books so that
the covers show, not just the spines.*

Dramatic Play (*Housekeeping*)

Equipment:

*Play stove/sink combination
Doll bed, blankets
Small table and chairs
Sturdy doll high chair
Large, unbreakable mirror
Two toy telephones*

*Dolls
Shelf for food boxes, shoes
    and purses, etc.
Dress up clothes
Play props such as pots and
    pans, plastic dishes*

Put out only a few easy to put on dress-up clothes and change them from week to week. A mug rack attached to the wall works well for hanging up dress-up clothes. Perhaps you can put some "kitchen" wall paper on the lower part of the wall, or on the backs of shelves used as dividers. Use contact paper to make silhouettes of kitchen tools and other items which can be placed on shelves or hung on the peg-board backing of a set of shelves used as a divider.

Fine Motor Development Center (*Manipulatives*)

Equipment:

>*Toddler size plastic fit-together toys of several types, such as: waffle blocks; pounding benches; rubber peg boards and large pegs; nesting cups; stacking rings.*
>*Table blocks*
>*Wooden inlay puzzles, starting with single piece, and growing in complexity*
>*Puzzle rack*
>*Shelf*
>*Low table*

Put a picture of each toy on the shelf where it is to be put away by the child. Toys with many pieces such as your fit-together toys could be stored in a box with a hole in the lid. Since children so enjoy sticking things through holes, they might be more cooperative at clean-up time. Lunch boxes are also fun for storing manipulatives. Although children like to play with these toys on the floor, providing a table can cut down on toys being scattered and stepped on. A low table, 8–12" off the floor is ideal. Children like to kneel on the floor and play with the toys at the table. Try removing the tubular legs from commercially produced tables, and put crutch tips over the bottoms of the remaining tubes.

Gross Motor Play Area

Equipment:

A safe indoor climber designed for toddlers	*A variety of balls*
	Collapsible tunnel
Safety mat under climber	*Push toys and pull toys*
Riding toys for indoors as well as outdoors	*Rocking boat*

You need space in this part of the room. Try making a "track" for the riding toys, if you have space, and perhaps dividing off the area somewhat, so the riding toys don't invade the rest of your room. Use tape to make "parking spaces" for riding toys against a wall. Push toys and pull toys could be hung up high on a peg board for storage if space is at a premium.

Science Center

Equipment:

Table
Classroom pet in cage, such as a guinea pig or fish
Sensory materials—things to touch, smell, listen to
Pictures of animals

Involve children in the care of the classroom pet for maximum learning value. Make sure children do not harass the pet. Use the table as a display area for interesting objects from nature as well as other sensory objects for children to discover and explore. Change the objects frequently to keep interest high.

Sensory Activities Interest Center

Equipment:

> *Sand/water table or dish pans*
> *Play equipment such as plastic containers of all shapes and sizes, plastic bottles, funnels and plastic toys*
> *Plastic smocks for water play*
> *(Clay, playdough, etc. could be offered here, at a table, as well as your art center.)*

You can change materials from week to week. Possibilities: water, sand, cornmeal, rice, playdough, shaving cream. Keep the various toys for such play in labelled containers. Rather than putting out all the toys at once, which can be overwhelming to a child, try putting out just a few choices and changing them from day to day. For example, put basters, plastic eye droppers and bowls in your water table one day; funnels, plastic bottles and cups another day. Try putting individual dish pans for each child inside the water table. This gives each child his own space and also cuts down on the spread of germs. If you don't have a water table, put dish pans inside a small plastic wading pool on a low table. Spills will go into the wading pool instead of onto the floor (for the most part).

ROOM ARRANGEMENT—DIVIDE AND ORGANIZE

Where you place the various "interest centers" in your room depends on several things—where the water source is, the shape of your room and the placement of carpeting and hard flooring. It makes sense to have messy areas, eating, art and sand and water play over hard flooring. If your room is entirely carpeted, you might consider putting large sheets of vinyl on the floor in these areas to simplify clean-up. You also need to be able to supervise well and have no "blind spots" in the room. Low dividers can effectively divide the space for children, still allowing adults to see in.

Furniture such as shelving, cubbies, small panel screens or a couch can be used as room dividers. Office dividers can also be used. Why bother? We know that toddlers are easily distracted by other children. If they are out of the direct line of sight of other children, they may play with greater concentration.

Children might be less likely to carry toys all over the room if the space is divided and it is clear where everything belongs. They will start to think of certain toys belonging in certain areas of the room. It will certainly help at clean-up time, which can become a large-scale sorting activity.

Ideas for Room Dividers:

- Low shelving with backs. This is the ideal room divider, because it gives you double use. While it divides your space, you have the advantage of storage to help you keep organized. Peg-board backs can be used to hang up objects, such as dress-up clothes or small toys, for the interest centers they face. Glue felt on the back of the shelf and you have a built-in felt board for a language area. Pictures and children's art work can be displayed at children's eye-level on the back of shelves. Hinged shelf storage units have the advantage of stability when you open them to an L position, and they give you two "walls."

- Area rugs. A change in the flooring helps differentiate space for young children. A large area rug is especially good for establishing a "circle time" space in the room. When you tell children to come and "sit on the rug," it is very concrete—they know what to do.
- Hanging dividers. If you have a dropped ceiling, you can hang things from it fairly easily. An attractive, partially transparent shower curtain makes a great divider.

SIX PACK RING DIVIDER

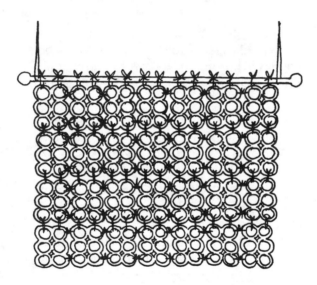

Materials:

> *Plastic six-pack rings from soft drink cans*
> *Yarn*
> *Crepe paper streamers (optional)*
> *Curtain rod*

Ask parents to help you collect plastic six-pack rings. Use short pieces of yarn to tie these together lengthwise and sideways so they cover the area you want to divide. Then suspend the curtain rod from the ceiling and hang the rings from it. You have an effective divider you can see through for good supervision. If you wish the divider to be more solid, you can weave the crepe paper streamers through the rings.

FOLDING SCREEN

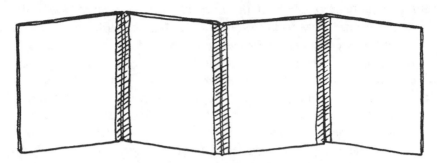

Materials:

> *Sturdy cardboard panels from a large box*
> *Duct tape—or any wide, flexible tape*
> *Wall paper or colored contact paper*

Cut four panels of cardboard which are exactly the same size and shape. Tape them together along their long edges, leaving about half an inch between panels so that they can be folded, accordion-style. (Put tape on both sides. Fold the panel before putting on the second piece of tape to be sure you allow enough give.) Cover the panels with wallpaper or contact paper. Stand this screen up in a zig-zag formation for stability.

STAYING ORGANIZED

It helps tremendously to have good storage containers for everything in your classroom and a clearly-marked place for everything. Store materials close to where they are to be used. It gives children a sense of control when they know where things go and where to find things. Plastic see-through boxes make good storage for manipulatives and art supplies. The child can see what is inside them to find what he needs.

PICTURE LABEL THE ROOM

Materials:

> *Pictures of toys*
> *Clear self-adhesive vinyl*

Find a picture of each toy and attach the picture to the place where the toy goes in the room. Old equipment catalogs are a good source of these pictures, or the box the toy arrived in. Lacking these, draw a picture of the toy and color it, or use photographs. Attach these pictures to the shelf, using clear contact paper which extends beyond the picture about half an inch on all sides.

Now you can play a game with the children. Gather several toys from different parts of the room. One at a time, ask children, "Where does this toy go? Can you find the picture of this toy in our room?" Then follow the child you select to the picture he chooses. Help him compare the real object to the picture. This is also a cognitive activity because the child is seeing a symbol (the picture) that represents the real thing. (Cognitive)

SPACES AND PLACES

Starting out with your basic, square room, see how many interesting "nooks and crannies" you can create for children to crawl into and on. As part of their "sensori-motor" period of development, children this age are endlessly exploring where they can fit, and different positions they can be in. They especially enjoy small, enclosed spaces. It is also important to allow children opportunities to be in places by themselves, and not always be part of the larger group. It could be as simple as a blanket over a table, or put up a small tent or tepee in one part of the room. It is likely to be used for dramatic play as well as a hide-away. Many toddler classrooms have a large commercially manufactured plastic fit-together cube or low climber that children love to crawl into. Throw a blanket or sheet over it for added drama.

BIG BOX = SMALL ROOM

Materials:

> *Large cardboard box, such as an appliance box. (Appliance stores or moving companies might give you used ones.)*
> *Wallpaper or contact paper*

Create a "room" by cutting a door and window out of the box. Wallpaper the inside to add extra strength to the box. You could also wallpaper the outside. One teacher glued egg cartons the children had painted all over the outside of such a box, making the box even more sturdy.

CARPETED BARREL

Materials:

Large cardboard barrel
Carpet samples
Glue
Cutting tool (use away from
*   children)*

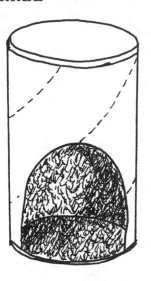

A large, sturdy cardboard barrel can become a special hide-away. Clean out of the barrel any residue of its former contents. Cut a round door near the bottom. Carpet the inside of the barrel with carpet scraps, gluing it onto the floor and sides. (Great addition to your book area.)

A STEP UP TO SEE OUT

Many toddler programs have windows that are too high for children. Have a handyman or carpenter build you a sturdy step for children to climb up on that will elevate them enough to be able to look out of the window. Ideally it should be wide enough to accommodate several children. Put railing guards on the side. This piece of equipment addresses two natural urges of toddlers— climbing and looking out of the window to see what is going on.

A "SOFT SPOT" FOR TODDLERS

An environment for toddlers and two-year-olds should be a place that is comfortable and warm for children and adults alike. Try adding some more soft things and see what it does to add calmness and comfort to your room. Create a "soft area." It doesn't have to be elaborate and can usually be pulled together from donated materials. You probably won't want to have *all* of the items listed below. See what you have around and what you can obtain inexpensively. Possibilities:

- Pillows, bolsters of different shapes and a mattress or thick foam pad could be covered with coordinating fabric to accent the color scheme in your room.
- A well-constructed beanbag chair is a nice addition, especially one covered with velour or corduroy or fake fur. Check the chair often to see that the seams are solid and none of the styrofoam beads inside can leak out. Or, consider filling the chair with foam rubber stuffing.
- An old water bed adds softness and warmth—an unbeatable combination. A flannel sheet covering would be nice.
- A rocking chair qualifies as a "softness" item, especially if it has a soft pad on it.
- A soft couch or easy chair would be great if they have washable covers.
- Hang a fabric "canopy" to lower the ceiling and create a soft top to your space.
- A shaggy area rug could make the floor soft.
- Blankets, quilts, large pieces of fake fur fabric, and samples of velvet or satin would add coziness.
- Your adopted stuffed animals could find a home here. Can you find some real big ones?

- Books, soft music, and other "quiet toys" such as a flannel board might be here.
- Soft lighting would add to the calmness of the atmosphere.
- Don't forget the most important thing of all—a nice soft lap!

DECOR

Your environment should be attractive and appealing to children, but beware of making it over-stimulating. Too many bright colors, shapes and busy patterns can be tiring over a period of hours. Try to create a balance. Neutral walls and flooring allow you to highlight materials of interest.

Hang pictures for children at child eye-level. Decorations meant for adults should be at adult eye-level. If you have trouble with children picking away and tearing pictures at their level, first simply try training them not to do that. Take them over to the damaged decoration and explain that it is not for tearing. Let them help you tape it back together. Then give the child something else to tear. If this doesn't work, you might put pictures behind plexiglass frames that are mounted low on the wall, or cover decorations with transparent contact paper.

Many people like to decorate toddler rooms with large pictures of cartoon characters. In actuality, these really mean very little to toddlers, although they may learn to name the character. (Is that so important?) Pictures of objects, people and scenes are meaningful to children. Photographs of themselves are especially interesting. Try to find pictures of people that represent all races, especially those represented by the children in your class.

You can have posters made relatively inexpensively from colored slides or 35 mm negatives. Check with your professional photo processing store. Take pictures of your children engaged in typical play activities, such as feeding dolls, playing with playdough or water, painting, building with blocks, etc. Make the best shots into posters and hang them in the part of the room where they were taken. Under each poster you can list the learning value for this type of play for the edification of any visiting adults.

THE OUTDOOR PLAY SPACE

Outdoor play time is extremely important for energetic toddlers and two year olds. It can also be a prime learning area of your environment. The wonderful thing about your outdoor space is that it changes more than the inside. Help children notice the changes. There may be snow one day. There may be puddles. Look at the sky for clouds, birds, airplanes, color. Notice wind, temperature, insects. You never quite know what wonders will greet you out there. Become childlike in your delight in this special part of your environment. Make it a challenge to see how many ways you can improve and enrich your outside play space. If you are a family child care provider, you can do wonders with a back yard.

Take a good look at the sensory aspects of your outside space. Outdoors, there are many exciting things to see, hear, smell and touch. You have nature: the sun and shadows, the sounds and smells of trees and the wind; bird songs, butterflies, the textures of grass. What else can you add? (Refer to the "Sensory" section of the "Creative" chapter for specific ideas.)

Sand Area

Your sand area is one of the most important parts of your outdoor environment. Sand play, difficult to offer children indoors, gives toddlers and two-year-olds numerous important learning opportunities and outlets for dramatic play. (See *The Outside Play and Learning Book* in the resource section at the end of this chapter for many specific sand play activities.) A great sand area is relatively easy to install, and will enhance any outdoor space. You need some type of border to keep the sand in. Large, smooth rocks are one possibility, or a wooden frame of some sort. Make it as large as your space will allow, so several children can play in it at one time. The type of sand available from building supply sources is much better than fine beach sand, which clings to clothing and does not mold well. You might provide a small broom with the handle cut down so that the children can help sweep up the sand that spills onto sidewalks.

Water Play

Water play in warm weather is endlessly interesting to toddlers and two-year-olds. Avoid wading pools though, because they are unsanitary for children in diapers. Instead, bring your water table outside, or simply offer water in dishtubs. A trickling hose is fascinating.

Climbing

Climbing is a major compulsion for this age group, so be sure to have safe and interesting climbing spaces in your outdoor environment. *Climbing structures do not have to be high in order to challenge toddlers.* Even low climbers should have soft, cushioning materials underneath. Children can practice different skills on steps, ramps and tires, which also add variations in elevation. Steps should be wide and low. There should be large platforms at the top of the steps so several children can congregate and there is room to sit down and turn around. A wide, low slide and a short tunnel to crawl through are good additions. There are more and more excellent manufactured climbers designed for toddlers.

Swinging

Swings should be placed in a spot that is away from the main flow of foot traffic on the playground, and far enough from the fence or building so that they would not hit these if the child is swinging high. Use horizontal tire swings or soft, sling-type seats rather than hard seats. Swings require constant adult supervision, because children *will* walk right in front of them.

Riding Toys

Toddlers dearly love pushing themselves along on low wheel toys. You will need a hard surface for riding toys, either a patio or a wide path. If you are building in a riding toy trail (not a terribly expensive project) design a trail that *goes somewhere* such as in a large circle, rather than just a straight line.

RESOURCES

Books:

Greenman, Jim, *Caring Spaces, Learning Places—Children's Environments that Work.* Exchange Press, 1988.

This is an inspiring book full of practical ideas and philosophies. It should really be in the library of every child care center.

Miller, Karen, *The Outside Play and Learning Book*. Gryphon House, Inc., 1989.
This book has a whole chapter on outside environments for infants and toddlers and other chapters on sand play, water play and snow. There are numerous outdoor play activities appropriate for toddlers and twos throughout the book.

Video Tape:

Jones, Elizabeth and Elizabeth Prescott, *Environments for Young Children*. NAEYC #806, $39.
This excellent video tape has an exercise in which Elizabeth Prescott "pretends" she wants to create an environment for children to foster *dependence* rather than independence. They then discuss the opposite, how to create an environment and learning program for fostering independence and initiative on the part of children.

CHAPTER 2

Becoming Active Thinkers

Cognitive activities involve the mental processes that give order to the world. Children are actively creating a mental "framework" into which they fit new knowledge as it comes along.

As a starting point, toddlers are driven to gain "physical knowledge" of the universe—to learn about things using all of their senses. Our world is filled with millions of fascinating objects. Toddlers are on a quest to fully examine each of them, and find out what they are good for! In their seemingly endless gross motor explorations, toddlers are going *in* and *out* and *under* things, gaining "body knowledge" or "internal knowledge" even before they learn the vocabulary words to represent these spacial concepts.

Cognitive activity is also learning about the relationships between objects. Older children sort things into groups, arrange things according to size, volume, length or weight, and actively compare objects. Toddlers and two-year-olds endlessly explore and experiment, in what may look like very random playing. What fits inside of what? What things go together?

Part of the process of cognitive development is learning "causality," what happens when you act on things. In *Things to Do with Toddlers and Twos* there is a whole chapter of "cause and effect" activities for children to have fun with. A few more are included in this chapter.

Ultimately, cognitive behavior is learning to engage in abstract thinking, retaining a mental image of something that is not right there in front of you. All the peek-a-boo variations fall into this category. Also involved in abstract thinking is representing things with symbols. Symbols do not, at this stage, mean letters and numbers, but seeing that a picture of something represents a real object. Children also use objects to represent something else, a different type of symbol, as in dramatic play (next chapter).

Really, all of education is the process of broadening one's mental framework as we assimilate new information. It's a life-long process that has many of its very active beginnings in early toddlerhood.

EXPLORING OBJECTS

Just watch what a toddler does when she encounters a new object. After putting it in her mouth, she will probably turn it around to see all sides, shake it to see if it makes a sound, bang it on the floor, put it on her head, try to get inside of it, throw it . . . in short, do everything she can think of with the object. This is her way of learning about the object.

This type of exploration is the same thing we would all do if we found ourselves in some strange and unfamiliar universe. Once we felt safe, we would try to figure out what everything was good for and how to use it to our advantage.

It is the beginning of concept development for toddlers. Before they learn the names of shapes and colors and other concepts, they simply have to be exposed to many examples and play with them. They gain the internal knowledge first, through their senses, and later learn the labels that go with them and figure out what categories they fit into.

One way an adult can support this kind of learning is to give the child many interesting things to examine over time, and talk about the objects, adding word labels to what the child is experiencing.

CONTAINER COLLECTION

Materials:

Interesting containers of all types such as purses, boxes, washed out milk jugs, tissue boxes, egg cartons, etc.
Interesting things to fill containers with such as macaroni, cotton balls, large pegs, smaller boxes, plastic eggs, etc.

Let the children have fun filling the containers and dumping them out again. They are learning about "inside" and "outside," what fits into what, and many other things. (Physical—Fine Motor)

NOTICING SIMILARITIES

As children gain experience playing randomly with objects, they begin to notice similarities in objects, and which things are the "same." There are many simple matching activities you can do that might interest toddlers. These activities involve looking closely at something and noticing attributes. Do these activities if they seem fun for toddlers, but don't force them if the child would rather play with the objects in some other way.

JUICE CAN LIDS MATCHING GAME

Materials:

Lids from frozen juice cans with pull-tape openers
Enough stickers to have one for each lid (two of each)
Spray paint (optional)
Box with lid (optional)

Spray paint the lids on both sides and let them dry. (Optional) Put a sticker on each lid. Cut a slot of a size that the lids will

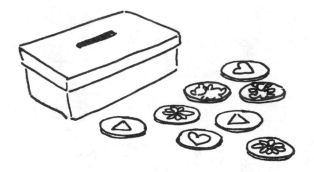

*fit through in the cover of the box and use the box for storage.
See if the children can find the matching pairs of stickers on the
lids. When they are through playing, let children put the lids
through the slot in the box cover to put them away.*

SOCK MATCHING GAME

Materials:

    *Adult socks with interesting patterns and colors, (one pair for
       each child in your group)*
    Bag

*Put one sock of a pair on each child's foot, over the shoe. Put
the other socks in the bag. Pull out one at a time and ask who
has one that is the same as this. Then let the child pull the matching*

sock over his other foot. Talk about the distinctive colors and patterns of each sock as you play the game. Later let children play with this sock collection by themselves. See if they play the game with each other spontaneously. (Language)

Activities related to noticing similarities in *Things to Do with Toddlers and Twos:* pp. 90, 91.

CONSERVATION ACTIVITIES

The term "conservation" when connected with cognitive development means that the child learns that the quantity of a material can remain the same even though the shape may change. To a young child, the substance seems to change in quantity as it changes in shape. A child will insist that there is more juice in a tall, skinny glass than in a short, wide glass. A flat pancake of clay will look like more than that same clay rolled into a ball. Over time (at age four or five), with lots of experience reversing and "undoing" their actions, the child will come to realize that the quantity stays the same. Do not try to explain this to toddlers or try to teach it in any way. Simply give them lots of experience with clay, playdough, sand, water and other changeable substances.

POKE, POUND AND ROLL

Materials:

> *Playdough, clay or plasticene.*
> *Objects to poke into it, which would make an interesting pattern such as plastic hair curlers, milk jug lids, tape spools, small plastic animals, a spiral notebook spring.*

Children enjoy playing with any clay-like material—including playdough, potters' clay and plasticene (modelling clay). Try to offer a variety over time. While they play with these wonderful materials, rolling snakes, smashing flat pancakes, wadding it back into a ball, they are learning to change the shape of a substance. Do not encourage children to make something from the clay or dough. Instead, just let them enjoy poking interesting things into it, noticing patterns, and pounding and rolling it. Children like knowing that they can change something. In the process they are developing their hand muscles (Physical—Fine Motor)

HOMEMADE PLAYDOUGH

There are many recipes for homemade playdough. Here is my favorite. It will last a long time if you keep it in a covered container in the refrigerator when not in use:

Mix together in a pot:

> *4 cups flour*
> *2 cups salt*
> *4 tablespoon cream of tartar*
>
> *4 cups water with food coloring in it*
> *2 tablespoons oil*

Cook over medium heat, stirring constantly until stiff. Let cool and knead. You could also add a few drops of various cooking extracts for interesting fragrances.

Playing with Sand

A well-enriched sand play area is an essential part of a good toddler program. Children learn about shapes and volume when they pour sand from one container into another. There are many sand activities throughout this book. Remember these two things about sand play:

- Have an interesting variety of "found" materials available for children to play with. If you have many kinds of containers to fill and dig with, children will absorb concepts of shape, size and volume.
- Play there yourself and model the different things one can do with sand. "Beginning diggers" will have great fun exploring sand on their own, but will also pick up ideas from you and other children. The more interesting things they know to do with sand, the less likely they are to eat or throw it. (Social. Guidance.)

SAND BOX SIFTING

Materials:

Purchased sand sifters with different size holes and/or kitchen sifters, colanders, pieces of screen of different size mesh, edges taped.

Using sifters, children learn a little bit about the sizes and shapes of objects and what will fit where. Let children enjoy sifting gravel, twigs and leaves out of their sand box. To make it even more fun, you can spray paint small stones and bury them in the sand box for children to "discover" as they sift.

Additional activities related to conservation in *Things to Do with Toddlers and Twos:* pp. 11–13; 56; 59–61.

REVERSIBILITY

"Reversibility" is another cognitive concept children discover on their own. They figure out that they can "undo" certain things or change them back to the way they were. This is essential if they are to learn the concept of "conservation" described above. Simply pouring substances back and forth between two differently shaped containers gives them some experience, as does the following type of activity. Think of your own variations.

PULL THROUGH BOX

Materials:

> *Cardboard box*
> *3 pieces of soft rope about 3*
>   *feet long each*
> *Scissors*

Make three sets of holes on opposite sides of the box, about ½ inch in diameter. String the rope pieces through holes on opposite sides of the box so they hang out both sides. Tie knots in the ends of the rope pieces so they cannot be pulled all the way through. Let the child pull on one end of the rope to make the other end shorter. For variety, tie small toys onto the ends of the clothesline pieces so they go up and down when the ropes are pulled.

PART-WHOLE AND SPACIAL RELATIONSHIPS

When a child learns to recognize that things are made up of many separate parts, it later becomes easier to see that words are made up of individual sounds represented by letters, and that sets of objects have individual components.

LOOKING THROUGH

Materials:

A washed out plastic bleach bottle with the bottom cut off.

When the child has become bored with putting the bleach bottle on his head like a hat, show him, if he hasn't discovered it already, how to look through the bottle from both ends. He will see his environment in a whole new way. If he puts his eye up to the small end, he'll see lots. If he puts his face into the large end, he'll see only a very small part of the room.

Children will also enjoy looking through paper towel tubes. For variety, put colored cellophane over one end, securing it with a rubber band, so the world will change color when the child looks through.

WHO'S IN THERE?

Materials:

> *File folder*
> *Picture of some popular television or cartoon character with*
>   *which children would be familiar*
> *Glue*
> *Scissors*

Glue the picture on the inside of the file folder. Cut little "doors" in the cover over particular body parts of the character. Open one at a time and ask, "Who has feet like this?" Close it again, open another and ask, "Who has eyes like this?" Let the child choose which door to open. Open each door, and then let the child open the file folder to see the whole character at once. Add file folders with other characters from time to time.

Puzzles and Shapes

Have a good variety of single piece inset puzzles, and 3–5 piece puzzles in your classroom, as well as an assortment of slightly more difficult puzzles, because a few two-year-olds will be able to do more. Experience gives children a real added advantage. Keep a list of which children can do which puzzles in your room. Every now and then offer one that is slightly more challenging.

Working a puzzle is a memory game for a child as well as one of fine motor skill. A child will sometimes know which piece goes where in an inset puzzle before she can figure out exactly how to make it fit by turning it and adjusting it. Two-year-olds can usually do simple puzzles of three or four pieces as well as single piece inset puzzles. With multi-piece puzzles they quickly memorize where each piece goes in the larger cut-out hole, and how it must be positioned. As a child works a puzzle she also sees the concept that all the different parts make up the whole picture. Don't put a puzzle away because she has mastered it. She will enjoy doing it again and again (and exercise her memory in the process) before she becomes bored with it.

HOMEMADE BLOCK SHAPE PUZZLES

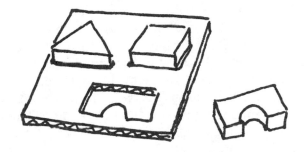

Materials:

> *Shallow box with a lid (such as a stocking box)*
> *Styrofoam meat tray, or thick piece of cardboard*
> *Large plastic shape blocks*
> *Pencil or pen*
> *Exacto knife (Do not use near children)*
> *Colored self-adhesive paper*

On a thick piece of cardboard, styrofoam meat tray, or the lid of a shallow box, trace around some shape blocks, or other toys with a distinct shape. Use an Exacto knife to cut out that shape and you have an instant puzzle. The child can put the toy itself in the hole, as well as the cardboard shape you have cut out, giving him two things to choose from to put in the hole—one flat, one three-dimensional. For greater durability, you could cover the puzzle base with contact paper, or put tape around the edges of the holes. Later, you could have the child match the flat shape to the three-dimensional shape. (Physical—Fine Motor)

Activities related to spacial relationships in *Things to Do with Toddlers and Twos:* pp. 89–92; 107; 112–115; 119–121.

CAUSE AND EFFECT

Let's go back and think about a baby. At first, things just "happen" to the baby. The baby cries because she is hungry and like magic, someone appears and makes her feel better. Before long, the baby learns to cry to make someone appear. Later, this same baby is lying in a crib randomly kicking when she suddenly notices the mobile above her jiggle and make some nice noises. She stops to concentrate and watch the movement. Soon the movement stops. Things get boring and the baby starts to kick again. Hey, it happened again, that stuff is jiggling! After a number of repetitions comes the big step. The baby kicks to see if she can make the mobile jiggle. It works! Do it again! It works again! Wow!

The child is now launched on one of the most compulsive drives that will carry her well through toddlerhood, the endless quest to make things happen and repeat the happenings. Thus, the toddler's love of flipping light switches, honking horns, flushing toilets, pushing levers, even perhaps hitting or biting. All these actions make other things happen. The baby feels powerful as she learns to make the world work for her. The child is no longer a passive being and is busy exploring her ability to impact the physical and social world.

Any activity you can think of in which the child can do something to get a dramatic visual or sound effect will appeal to a toddler. Possibilities are endless, but here are a few fun ones.

THREE PLASTIC BOTTLE TOYS

The following three "cause and effect" toys are all made from plastic bottles. It would be fun to have a whole set of these. The materials listed below cover all bottles.

Materials:

    3 plastic liter pop bottles and   *Tempera paint*
        caps   *Small plastic toys*
    Strong glue   *Yarn*
    Water   *Liquid dish detergent*
    Food coloring

1. COLORED BUBBLES BOTTLE. Fill a plastic pop bottle one third full with water. Add tempera paint and about ⅓ cup of liquid detergent. Glue on the cap. Let the child shake the bottle to make colored bubbles.

2. DANCING YARN BOTTLE. Put numerous pieces of yarn cut in short pieces (about 3 inches to 6 inches) into a plastic pop bottle. Fill the bottle with water. Glue on the cap. Let the child shake the bottle to make the yarn dance inside.

3. SWIRLING OBJECTS BOTTLE. Fill a plastic pop bottle half full with water. Add some food coloring. Then add small, light plastic toys, plastic sequins, beads, some things that float and some things that do not. Glue on the cap. Let the child shake the bottle to make the objects swirl around.

ROLLING THINGS DOWN A RAMP

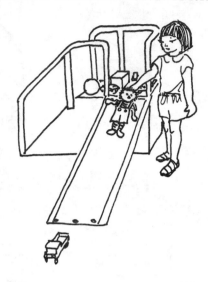

Materials:

> *A ramp of some sort—an indoor or outdoor slide, a large wedge-shaped block, or a wide board propped up on one end.*
> *A collection of toys to try to roll down the ramp such as toy cars, stuffed animals, various balls, a block, large pegs, wooden beads, bean bags.*

Let the child put each object, one at a time, at the top of the ramp and see what happens. Later, try changing the angle of the ramp (if it is not a built in slide) and make it less steep. Do some things stop sliding? You will find that children play this game quite independently, without a lot of adult guidance.

Activities related to cause and effect in *Things to Do with Toddlers and Twos:* pp. 1–9; 12–17; 22–27; 30; 34; 38; 42–44.

OBJECT PERMANENCE

"Object permanence" is the term used to describe a child's ability to retain a mental picture of something when he cannot see it, and realize that things continue to exist, even when they are out of sight. This ability begins in the last part of the first year. If an object rolls out of sight of a baby of six or seven months, the child will seem to forget about it. He will not look for it or try to get it back. Somewhere between eight and ten months, the child remembers the object and tries to find it again. This is very exciting, because it is the beginning of abstract thought. All through the toddler years, children will enjoy "testing" this, and enjoy making things appear and disappear. Remember also that all types of hide and seek games are really variations on "peek-a-boo" and are therefore a big hit with toddlers and two-year-olds.

MUSIC BOX HIDE AND SEEK

Materials:

Wind-up music box or transistor radio

Try hiding something that makes a noise like a radio or wind up music box and see if children can follow the sound to find it.

Pockets, Pockets, Pockets!

Toddlers are fascinated by pockets of all types. They *hide* things which can be discovered. Sew pockets in dress up clothes. A pocket collection would be great fun.

POCKETS COLLECTION BOOK

Materials:

 Old clothing with pockets   *Needle and thread*
 Fabric   *Small toys*
 Scissors

 Make a cloth book out of the fabric scraps. Cut the pockets out of old clothing and sew them to the pages of the cloth book. Put small toys inside the pockets. As the child turns the page of the book (a peek-a-boo activity in itself) he can then take the toys out of the pockets and play with them, gaining a little fine motor practice in the process. When the child is finished playing with the toys, let him put them back in the pockets again. (Physical— Fine Motor)

 Keep your eye open for other interesting pockets to add to your collection as time goes by. Purses and wallets have special pockets. Add some play money.

AN ENVELOPE COLLECTION

Envelopes are a special kind of pocket.

Materials:

 Envelopes of all types to fill. Different sizes of padded envelopes, window envelopes, square envelopes, long envelopes
 Laminated pictures and other interesting things to put in envelopes
 Junk mail

Let children open your junk mail and play with it. Put special pictures in the other envelopes and bring them out at special times. You could encourage children to talk about the pictures (Language) or just let them have fun taking them out of the envelopes and putting them back in again. (Physical—Fine Motor)

BURIED TREASURES

Materials:

 Small plastic toys
 Sand or cornmeal to dig in
 Spoons to dig with

What fun it is to discover some surprise while you are digging! Simply bury small toys in the sandbox outside. Indoors, children enjoy digging with small spoons in tubs of cornmeal. A set of plastic dinosaurs—although toddlers cannot understand what they are—seem to be especially fun for this activity. Children will also enjoy re-burying these things—an elaborate game of peek-a-boo! Perhaps you could challenge children to bury things in the sand before you go inside for lunch, and let them dig them up again when you go outside in the afternoon. It adds "adventure" to the sand box. (Creative—Sensory)

Activities related to object permanence in *Things to Do with Toddlers and Twos:* pp. 98–108.

SYMBOL TO THING

A picture is a symbol of something real. Comparing pictures to the real things they represent gives children practice with symbols. Letters and numbers are other symbols they will begin to learn about later in their preschool years.

PICTURE TO REAL THING GAME

Materials:

> *Old toy catalog that has*
> *pictures of some of the*
> *toys in your room*
> *Thin cardboard or heavy*
> *paper*
> *Clear contact paper*
> *Scissors*

Let children help you find pictures of toys in their room in the catalog. Cut the pictures out, mount them on the cardboard and cover with clear contact paper for durability. Then hand one of the pictures to a child and ask her to find that object in the room. The child is learning that a picture is a symbol that represents a real thing.

See if you can find pictures in magazines of other things you have in your room, even if they are not exactly the same, such as a clock, a rocking chair, a sink, a toilet, a plant. Can the child generalize from the picture and find the object that serves the same function in your room? (Language)

CONCEPTS OF TIME

Learning to understand concepts of time is another cognitive activity. It is certainly one way we organize our thoughts and our world.

Concepts like the days of the week and the months of the year are beyond toddlers. "Calendar" activities which might be appropriate for kindergarten classes are wasted on toddlers and two-year-olds. With effort, some young children can be taught to recite the days of the week in order, just as they can recite the alphabet or count to 20. But they might as well be asked to recite nonsense syllables—which they can also do. These concepts are still meaningless to them. As people around them use the names of the months and the days of the week in normal conversation, the child's awareness will increase and the concept will be more meaningful in a few years.

Even "yesterday," "today" and "tomorrow" are confusing, because they keep moving around! "Today" becomes "yesterday" with mysterious regularity!

A TWO-DAY PROJECT

To give children more practical experience with the concepts of today and yesterday, try doing a project that stretches over two days. On the second day, remember what you did "yesterday." For instance, you could have children paint rocks one day. The next day hide the rocks on the playground and let the children find them. Then let them wash off the paint with sponges. As they are washing the paint, you can say, "Remember, yesterday we painted these rocks. Today we found them and are washing the paint off again. Shall we paint them again tomorrow?"

Children can also begin to understand words such as soon, later, next, as they hear them in real-life situations.

A PHOTOGRAPHIC SEQUENCING GAME
Materials:

Camera and film   *Clear self-adhesive plastic*

Take pictures of the children engaged in all your daily routines and transitions: arrival time, saying good-bye to parents, washing hands, morning snack, bathroom time, play time, putting on outdoor clothing, playing outside, taking off outdoor clothing, setting the table, eating lunch, putting out cots, rest time, etc.

After these pictures are developed, you might encase them individually in clear self-adhesive plastic for durability. Younger toddlers will simply enjoy looking at them and identifying people they know. Your older two-year-olds might be able to arrange the pictures in the sequence of when they happen in your routine. Talk to them as they do this. What do we do first each day? What do we do after snack? Difficult concepts, the child will nevertheless enjoy lining up the pictures, whether he gets the sequence right or not. (Language, Program Management)

EXPANDING UNDERSTANDINGS

Children start with very narrow understandings of concepts. For instance, if a child has only seen one dog in his life, he will think all dogs look alike. The way children's understandings grow is by having many real-life experiences with the topic. There are ways to give children a variety of experiences with a topic, other than simply showing them many pictures, once the child has already been exposed to it. Here are just a few examples:

VISITING ANIMALS

Arrange for different animals to visit your class or playground. Survey parents to see what pets might visit. If children see five different dogs in a relatively short time, they will have a better understanding of what "dog" is. Sometimes local Humane Society programs or zoos have animals available to visit educational institutions. Is there a 4-H club in your area? Perhaps one of the children raising an animal would bring the animal by to show the children. Children learn much more seeing the "real thing" than from looking at pictures of animals.

FILE FOLDER PICTURE COLLECTIONS
Materials:

File folders   *Magazine pictures*

Glue one picture on outside of the file folder. Inside, glue many more pictures of the same type of object. A pick-up truck might be on the outside, and pictures of a moving truck, a dump truck, a garbage truck, a delivery truck and a car carrier might be on the inside. On another folder, a cat might be on the outside, and many different kinds of cats on the inside. (Language)

DOOR BOARD WITH A THEME

Materials:

> 2 pieces of posterboard
> Tape
> Glue
> A *number of pictures or photographs of the same subject (a dog, for example) from different angles.*

Cut a number of different "door flaps" in one piece of the poster-board. Make the flaps of different sizes to go with the pictures, and have some lift up, and some open sideways. Place this board over the second posterboard and lightly trace where the holes are. Then glue the pictures in place. When children see the subject from several different angles, or see several different types, their understanding of the concept will be strengthened. (Language)

CATEGORY SORTING POCKET CHARTS

Materials:

> Poster board   Index cards
> Staples or tape   Magazine pictures

Make a pocket chart by cutting a two-inch high strip from the long side of the posterboard and staple or tape it to the bottom of the larger piece. Place staples or tape at intervals to create pockets that index cards would fit into. Then find and cut out as many pictures of one kind of thing—babies, for instance, or dogs, or cats, or birds, or flowers—as there are pockets. Let the children put the pictures into the pockets and talk about them. (Language)

You could create a large number of these charts, adding one each week, perhaps, as you expose children to new concepts. Glue a picture of the category on each chart. Later you might pick two charts you have made and with which children are familiar, such as babies and dogs, and pull out all the cards and mix them. Challenge the children to put the cards back in the right chart. This then becomes an elementary classifying activity.

RESOURCES:

Singer, Dorothy G. and Tracey A. Revenson, *A Piaget Primer— How a Child Thinks*. New American Library. New York, 1978. This very readable book describes various aspects of children's development with easy to understand examples and the aid of cartoons.

CHAPTER 3

The Adventure of
Language Development

One of the most exciting things about working with toddlers and two-year-olds is watching the amazing development of language. The young toddler starts out with meaningful grunts and single word utterances. Before long you notice two-word combinations and then short sentences. It's truly one of the wonders of the human brain that such young children can learn to speak and incorporate the rules of grammar.

Of course, the child has been learning about language long before the sentences start coming. From the time the young crying baby is picked up and hears soothing remarks, and all through infancy, the child knows that sounds that mean things come from people. The child first understands intonation. A baby knows when someone is angry, frightened, or trying to make him smile. Soon particular words are understood—such as "ba-ba" for "bottle."

Language development does not happen in isolation. Children learn language through real experiences—it is a spontaneous process that goes on all the time. For that reason, adults who work with toddlers and twos should always be conscious of the words they use to describe what the child is experiencing and listen with special ears to the attempts the child makes to communicate.

For the most part, the activities in this chapter are "fun extras." *The bulk of the language learning in your program will come from the "real language" that goes on in everyday occurrences and your routine interactions with children.*

HOW CHILDREN LEARN TO UNDERSTAND AND TALK

Understanding

A child can often understand what you say long before he can speak sentences himself. It is a process, however, that goes on simultaneously with learning to talk, as children hear new words connected to things that interest them. The main way to increase children's understanding of words and concepts is to talk about what the child sees in front of her, and what is going on at the moment. Put verbal labels on what the child is tasting, touching, hearing, smelling and seeing. Describe what the child is doing. Use a normal tone of voice, speaking somewhat slowly, and with your best pronunciation.

Many people are impressed by early talkers. Early speech in itself, is not necessarily a sign of superior intelligence. More important is the indication that the child *understands* language.

Talking

Learning to speak is a different process from learning to understand. Children must learn to use the muscles of their mouths and throats to make just the right sounds. These sounds, furthermore, must come out in the right order to represent each different object or event. This starts in the first year when we hear the delightful "babbling," or "jargon talk" of infants. They are trying out all the different sounds they can make. Certain sounds will be reinforced by delighted adults—"ma-ma."

Children quickly find out that talking is a means to an end. They can use words to get a response from other people. They find out that producing the right sounds is a way to get an object they desire. You also see a bit of the delight of a puzzle solver. Children start pointing to and naming objects, almost as if to say, "Hey—I know the sounds that go with that thing!"

At this point, the adult can expand on the child's single-word utterances. The child points and says "kee." The adult says, "Oh yes . . . there is a kitty! Do you want to pet the kitty? The kitty is soft. Hear her purr." Child: "Puh." Adult: "Yes, she is purring. Purr, purr, purr." Before long the child starts combining two and then more words. "Kee puh." And you're off and running!

To encourage the child to use new speaking skills, wait—let the child talk. Give him time to get it out. Repeat his words, check for comprehension.

Of course, early pronunciations are often less than accurate. It can be an intriguing experience to be a stranger in a toddler classroom where the teacher knows the children well. Teachers, parents and older siblings can understand what is a mystery to other people. They listen carefully and with interest, and then "interpret" for the rest of the world, by using the toddler's phrases again in sentences of their own. At this point, do not be terribly concerned about mispronunciations. *Do* keep records of how the child commonly pronounces words.

Grammar

When children start combining words to make short sentences, we see the amazing acquisition of grammar. The child puts the words in the right order, and gradually learns such things as using the past tense of verbs and making the subject and verb agree. If you have ever studied a foreign language, you know how difficult this can be, and here we have two-year-olds simply "absorbing" it. Children's invented grammar is often more logical than "correct usage" of English, because they have not learned exceptions. For instance they figured out that adding an "-ed" to a word means it happened in the past. ("I petted the kitty.") So they add this -ed all the time: "I eated." "He goed away in his car." Likewise, they commonly add "s" to indicate more than one: "foots." You do not need to correct these "mistakes." Simply use correct grammar in your own speech and the child will gradually refine his usage.

Expand on Children's Attempts to Communicate

Expand "telegraphic speech." Young children start out talking leaving out the little words between, just like old time telegrams. "Want juice!" "Mommy car go." Listen with interest to what the child says and expand on the phrase in your response, modelling full sentences. "Oh, you want some of this red juice? I'll pour some in your glass." "Yes. Mommy's car is going out of the parking lot."

ACTIVITIES FOR LISTENING, UNDERSTANDING AND TALKING

PICTURE BOX

Materials:

5" × 8" file box	*Magazine pictures*
Index cards to fit in box	*Clear self-adhesive paper*
Index card file dividers	

Cut numerous small pictures of interesting, familiar objects from magazines and attach them to the index cards with the self-adhesive paper. (Children can help you find the pictures.) Later you might have children help you sort all these pictures into categories such as food, animals, cars, cartoon characters, men, women, children, clothing, machines, etc. Put a picture on a divider representing the categories and have the children help you file all of the pictures in the box. Place this box of pictures in your book corner for children to explore on their own, as well as with you. Add new

pictures from time to time, storing others, to keep interest high.
(Cognitive)

CATEGORY BOOKS

Materials:

Sandwich size zip closure   Thin cardboard
   bags   Scissors
Needle and thread   Magazine pictures

Sew three or four bags together on the end opposite the zip closure
to make a book. Cut pieces of cardboard to fit inside each bag to
stiffen the pages and form a background. With the children, find
pictures in magazines that are all of a particular type of thing—
dogs, cars, food or babies, for instance, and put them in the pages
of the book. The child absorbs language as you talk about what
you see. The child might also begin to understand the concepts
that things can be grouped together. Make a collection of this
type of book, perhaps adding one new category each week. (Cogni-
tive)

SURPRISE BAG CURRICULUM
Materials:

Large, opaque, brightly colored shopping bag

Every day, as you leave the house (or before children arrive, if
you are a home care provider), put some common household object

into the bag. At a given time each morning, say to the children, "I have a surprise for you in this bag." Slowly, and with drama, pull out the object. Help the children describe it and talk about what it is used for. When you put labels on a real object like this, the words are more likely to make sense to the child and be understood in other contexts later. Bring in a different object each day.

FLANNEL BOARD WORD GAME

Materials:

Flannel board
Pictures of common objects, backed with felt

Gather a small group of children. Spread out several pictures of different objects on the floor or table in front of your flannel board. Ask one child at a time (or have your puppet ask) to pick up a picture you name or describe. If the child does so correctly, she can put it on the flannel board. Adjust the complexity of your description for each child. When all the pictures are on the flannel board, point to one and see if a child can name it (productive language) before he takes it down. Later, let children play the game by themselves during free play time.

CREATE AND LISTEN TO STORY TAPES

Materials:

Cassette tape recorder/player

Make a recording of children's favorite stories, speaking slowly and clearly, with good expression. (Rehearse a couple of times first.) If you read the story from a familiar book, start playing the story without telling the children which one it is. Let them tell you which story they think it is when they have heard a little bit of it. They could then go and find the book on the bookshelf, and find the picture that represents the part the tape is talking about. (Put the tape player on "pause" to allow children time to do this.) This activity forces children to listen closely, and associate words with picture symbols. (Cognitive)

THE MOST WONDERFUL TEACHER IN THE WORLD

Gather the children around and tell a story about what your group of children did that morning, but frame the story in traditional story words: "Once upon a time, there was a very wonderful teacher . . . the most wonderful teacher in the world. Her name was Miss Elizabeth. She was very beautiful. She had soft, grey hair and the kindest eyes you ever saw. She also knew lots of wonderful things to do to have fun. And she had a great group of children. In fact, they were the most wonderful children in the world. There was a boy named Jamie who had light blond hair that was straight. And there was Amanda, who had dark brown skin and the most beautiful big, brown eyes you ever saw. Then there was Jeffrey. His hair was curly and dark brown. He was wearing a new pair of red sneakers. (Go on to describe each child in your group.) It was a beautiful morning in the spring. The sky was blue and the sun was shining and it was warm outside. (Describe the weather conditions of the day.) The children didn't even need to put on their jackets when they went outside. They had oranges and graham crackers for their morning snack and then decided to go outside to enjoy the nice weather. When they got out on the playground, what do you think they saw? . . ."

Simply describe all the events of your morning. You may find that children jump in to add details. This is great "receptive" language practice, because the words are connected to real experiences. This activity is good for the self-image of the teacher as well as the children. (Self)

By the way, this technique can work well with a child at home too. Tell a story about the most wonderful mommy, or daddy, in the world and the most wonderful child, and describe your home and the events of the morning. Suggest it to parents. (Families)

POCKET APRON

Materials:

> *A large apron*
> *Fabric*
> *Needle and thread*
> *Scissors*
> *Small objects and toys*

Sew as many pockets on your apron as you have children in your group. Put a small toy in each pocket. Wear the apron and invite each child, one at a time, to choose a pocket and take the toy or object out of it. Encourage the child to talk about the object and then let

the children play with all their objects. Later, let them put all
the objects back into the pockets again. To keep interest high,
change the objects in the pockets from time to time.

TELEPHONE CENTER

Materials:

Two or more toy or real telephones

*Place the phones on a shelf where children can reach them. Having
two phones will increase the chances of children talking to each
other. You could model this by picking up one receiver, dialing
a number and saying to a child, "It's for you," while pointing at
the other phone. Then try to have a phone conversation with the
child. If a child is missing a parent during the day, you could
pretend to call the parent at work, you taking on the voice of the
parent.*

PHOTO SEQUENCE CARDS

Materials:

Camera
Clear self-adhesive plastic

*Make your own book of real experiences children have had. Let
the children help you assemble the pictures in their proper sequence
in a photo album. Older children can dictate the words to describe
each photo. For instance, if you are planning a walk around the
block with them the photos might be: 1) you and the children
looking out of the window, 2) putting on coats, 3) going out of
the gate, 4) several pictures of things you saw and people you
met along the way, 5) returning to your building, 6) taking off
and hanging up coats, and 7) having snack. Children will enjoy
"reading" this type of book over and over again. Assembling the
photos in the right sequence and remembering the events are good
"cognitive" activities, and this is a delightful way to let parents
know what is going on in your program. Cooking projects, art
activities, cleaning an animal's cage, are other possibilities to
record in this way. (Cognitive; Families; Program)*

VIDEOTAPE YOUR DAY

Materials:

Video camera and tape   VCR

Produce a video tape of a typical day in your class. (Could you invite a friend or parent to be the "camera man?") Record children arriving and being greeted, and the rest of your day—snack, story time, play time, going outside, rest time, etc.) Later, show this to the children. Use the pause button to stop the tape and talk about what is going on in different scenes. What happened to Hank? Why is he laughing? Why do we all have our coats on? . . . etc. This is terrific for language development, the self-image of children, as well as describing your program to parents, and evaluating yourself. (Self; Families; Program; Professional.)

CIRCLE TIME

Circle time, small group time, story time—that bastion of traditional nursery school programs—can have its beginning in a program for two-year-olds. You are *introducing* the children to the concept of sitting down as a group and doing things together. Traditionally thought of as a special language development time, children also learn the social pleasure of being a valued member of a group.

Circle time can be difficult with younger children because their attention span is short, they are impulsive and they don't yet focus on others as much as older children do. If their language skills are low, it is even more difficult. Don't consider this an "essential" element of your program. If it just doesn't work with your group, you can always settle down with a few children at a time for a story or some focused activity while others play elsewhere. Please see the "Routines" chapter for hints for success.

POETRY

Young children greatly enjoy the sound of poetry—its rhythms and music. Poetry helps children learn to play with language and use it creatively, building on what they do naturally.

"Mother Goose" rhymes are a good place to start. Don't worry if children don't understand some of the words. It's the sound of the words that appeals. Also expose children to good modern poetry. *Read Aloud Rhymes*, edited by Jack Prelutsky, Random House is one excellent source. "Fingerplays," simple rhymes with hand movements, are another popular form of poetry to use with young children. Adding hand movements gives children a little bit of fine motor practice, and also helps them remember the words and sequence of the poem. *Hand Rhymes*, collected by Marc Brown, is one good source.

Introduce new rhymes to children every couple of weeks, or more often, if you feel your group can absorb them, but don't drop the old rhymes. Keep them alive by chanting them often in casual moments during the day. If appropriate, show the children pictures as you read a poem the first few times, act it out, use puppets, or invent hand motions to bring life and greater meaning to the rhymes. Send home a copy of the poem to parents.

Don't try to get children to memorize and recite poetry. That only adds unnecessary pressure that can even "turn children off" to poetry. Instead, just repeat favorite rhymes over and over again with obvious pleasure. You'll find that children join in automatically and will memorize parts of them over time.

Model creative language behaviors yourself. Make up your own chants and songs and poems to go along with routines of your day and spontaneous happenings in the classroom. Most of all, keep a playful spirit with poetry. Show your own obvious enjoyment of poems. Saying poems together is an enjoyable group experience that gives a child a feeling of belonging.

Notice it when spontaneous poetry comes from the children. "Listen . . . what Davie just said sounds like a poem. He said, 'Brmmm, brmmm, brmmm . . . the car went up the hill. Brmmm, brmmm, brmmm . . . down it came again.' I like your poem, Davie."

READING BOOKS TO TODDLERS

There are many reasons why well-chosen picture books are ideal for toddlers and two year olds. We know that a favorite word of two-year-olds is "surprise." Books are full of surprises! Every time you turn a page, there is a new surprise. We know that toddlers love anything on a hinge—any kind of flap. A book is really a system of hinges. We also know that very young children love playing peek-a-boo. Peek-a-boo is built into books. Listening to stories can increase children's comprehension of words and ability to follow a story line. Young children enjoy hearing the same book over and over again because, as they correctly predict story events, it gives them a sense of control. Let's not forget the social pleasure of snuggling in close to a favorite adult. Sharing a book is sharing an experience with friends. Probably most important, you are teaching them the love of books.

Techniques for Reading to Toddlers

- Flop down and cuddle up in a comfortable place and read to one or two children at a time. They can see the illustrations and writing well and can interrupt and participate. If you read to a larger group of five or six children, make sure each child is comfortable and can see the pictures.
- Read slowly and with appreciation. Don't rush through a book. Present it like a special gift. Show the children the cover and tell them what the title is. When you turn each page, pause a moment to look at the illustrations with the children. Read the words slowly and clearly. Pause after each page, in case children want to add something.
- Let your finger point to the words you read. This gives the message that those little black marks tell you what to say.
- Leave out words. As you read a familiar book to a child, pause in the middle of the sentence and let him supply the missing word. Also encourage the child to add sound effects. This technique gives him a feeling of "owning" the story, an important pre-reading attitude.
- As you look at a familiar book with a child, make deliberate mistakes. Point to a picture of a dog and say, "Look at this pretty kitty." Or change a familiar phrase. "So the little pig said, 'Sure, Mr. Wolf . . . come right in!' " Let the child "catch you" and correct the error, or giggle and enjoy the change.
- When you find yourself with a few free moments, ask a child to tell you the story of one of her favorite books.
- Think out loud. Share with the children simple thought processes that typically go along with reading a good story. After you read a page, say what might be in a reader's mind. "Hmmm

. . . I wonder what will happen next. I guess I'll turn the page so we can see." The idea is to be a model, not just saying the words that are printed but also what the reader is thinking. Be sure to model the satisfaction at the end of the story. Talk about what parts of the story you liked the best, when you were worried, etc.

• By all means, if possible, grant children the wonderful request, "Read it again."

Selecting Books for Very Young Children

Libraries and book stores offer you many fine choices of books that your children will enjoy. Bring in new books to share with children frequently, making use of your public library, if necessary. Try to find some simple picture books with one photo or illustration on each page. Toddlers will enjoy putting their fingers on each picture and naming the object. You can add descriptive words. As children progress in language skill, you can also use simple story books. Toddlers like books about familiar things—pets, families, vehicles. They are also intrigued with books that have animals as characters. Look for books with repetitive phrases so the children can predict and join in. Check to see that people of different races or cultures are represented respectfully and not in stereotypical ways. Try to find books about all kinds of people including old people and those with disabilities. Try to link books you present to children with their real life experiences—birthday parties; petting animals; trucks. You can keep special books and library books on a "teacher shelf" and only make them available when you are there to supervise.

Make Some Books Available to Children All the Time

In your book corner, offer several books that are favorites of children and very familiar to them. Teach children to turn pages carefully and place books back on the shelf. To add durability, consider covering all the pages and the cover with clear self-adhesive plastic. Put out only a few books at a time. When there are too many books, children may become distracted and play with the books like objects, or simply dump them on the floor. Have a combination of homemade books made from photo albums or zip close bags sewn together, as well as commercial books.

USING PUPPETS

Puppets are almost universally appealing to young children. They are approachable, interesting and funny. What makes them so intriguing to children is that they know the puppets are not "real," and yet . . . they move and talk like real live things do.

There is a wide variety of beautiful commercial puppets available. However, homemade puppets work just as well and can have even more "personality." You can make a puppet out of almost anything. Draw a couple of eyes on a banana and talk for it in a funny voice, and children will listen with rapt attention. Sock puppets, puppets made from gloves, stick puppets, even finger puppets made from the fingers of old gloves will work.

While you can make some puppets available for children to put on and play with, it's a good idea to make one puppet a special "pet puppet" and only operate it yourself. Don't let children put it on. This will keep its personality intact. Give the puppet a name, a special voice, and a distinct personality. It can come out at certain times of day, like right before lunch, or during your circle time to talk to the children. Here are some fun things to do with a pet puppet:

MAKE A PUPPET HOME

Materials:

> *Box with lid that the puppet will fit inside*
> *Tempera paint and brushes*
> *Cotton or other soft materials*
> *A little blanket (piece of towel?)*

Let children paint the box. When the paint is dry use black paint or a marking pen to make a door and windows on the box to make it look like a house. Decorate further any way you wish. You could make a slanted roof with cardboard. You could print the puppet's name on the house. Put the soft material and blanket inside for "bedding." Keep your pet puppet in here when it is not in use. Let the children tuck him in. (Creative)

DESCRIPTIVE GREETINGS

Materials:

   Pet puppet

When the puppet first comes out, let him greet each child by name and describe the clothing the child is wearing. Or, play a guessing game, having the puppet describe the clothing each child is wearing until the children guess who it is. Then that child gets a hug from the puppet. (Self)

SILLY QUESTIONS

Materials:

   Pet puppet

The puppet asks the children (individually, or in a small group) silly questions ("Do cars drink milk?") or describes things incorrectly ("You have such lovely green hair.") This tickles the children's sense of humor, and the children can correct the puppet and display their vocabulary and knowledge.

TEACH YOUR PUPPET "BIG" AND "LITTLE"

Materials:

   Pet puppet
   Small ball

Your pet puppet is not very bright. He appears in front of the children with a very small ball, and says, "Look at the great big ball I found!" The children (or you) will inform him that that is not a big ball at all, in fact, it is a very little ball. The puppet acts confused. You can say "Gosh, puppet, you don't seem to know about big and little, do you? Well, we'll help you." Then have children, one at a time, get things that are either big or little (you tell them which to get) and bring them back to the group and sort them into two piles, to teach the puppet the difference. You can vary this activity to explore other contrast concepts such as rough and smooth, hard and soft, light and heavy, etc.

GATHER THINGS

Materials:

   Pet puppet   *Objects from around the room*
   Large bag

*The puppet could explain to the children that he "needs" certain
things (because he's going on a trip, is making something, is bored
in his house, etc.) Let him describe objects in the room he wants
and have children go and get these objects for him. Perhaps each
day, before he "goes to bed" he could ask for one object to keep
him company. Adjust the complexity of the puppet's descriptions
to the child he is talking to. Name the object for children with
lesser language skills. "Please bring me the ball." For more ad-
vanced children, describe the object. "I want a thing that is round
and red and bounces." He could also collect things that have a
certain attribute—for instance, he could ask children to bring him
soft things.*

PUPPET SHOW AND TELL

Materials:

   Pet puppet   *Interesting object*

*Let the puppet bring out a "surprise" object to show the children—
something interesting and new, such as an egg beater or a wind-*

up alarm clock. Let the puppet and the children describe the object and use it together.

PUPPET SAYS

Materials:

  Pet puppet

This is a simplified version of "Simon Says." Let the puppet pick one child at a time and tell the child to do one or two things. "Scratch your ear and turn around." "Put the red block under the chair." Children enjoy performing for the puppet, and are learning location words and listening skills in the process.

WHAT ARE APPROPRIATE PRE-READING ACTIVITIES FOR THIS AGE?

All the activities in this chapter are appropriate pre-reading activities for toddlers and two-year-olds. Before children can learn to read, they must be able to understand spoken language and express themselves. Reading to children from a wide variety of books shows them what books are for and that letters in groups represent sounds and concepts. You are also demonstrating an *attitude* about reading—that it is fun and useful.

Do you need to teach children their letters and shapes, and put flash cards in front of them? *No.* There is plenty of time to learn these things later in preschool and kindergarten. It is a rare child who grows up in our society who doesn't absorb these things from the environment. It doesn't *hurt* children to learn to recite the alphabet (a string of nonsense syllables at this age) and recognize letter shapes, as long as adults don't pressure and "drill" the child, but these are largely meaningless activities. Your time is much better spent on enriching the child's experience base and vocabulary, giving a child many opportunities to express himself, and engendering a love of books.

SPEECH AND HEARING SCREENING

We know that children learn language at different rates. Some precocious children are speaking full sentences at 18 months, while others are still uttering single words at 24 months. Pronunciation is likely to be very inaccurate much of the time. When is there cause for concern? Consult with your program director before expressing your concerns to the family and don't jump to conclusions. Record examples so you have specifics to go on.

- When a child is on target in every other area of development, but slow in speech development, parents need to rule out a hearing problem. A pediatric check-up can reveal a build up of fluid in the ears, a common concern for children in group child care situations. This is a serious problem and can have severe limiting effects on the development of intelligence if it goes undetected. It is generally correctable by tubes in the ears.

- When a two-year-old child does not seem to understand the meaning of common words, it may be a signal to have the child's hearing tested. Make sure you know the child and the family well (Is English spoken in the home?) and the child has been in your program at least a month or two, because the child may just be withdrawing as a way of adjusting to you.

- A two-year-old who understands words but does not articulate clearly is not a candidate for speech therapy. Simply model consistent correct pronunciation yourself and the child's speech will gradually refine itself. If severe mispronunciations continue after the child is three, it may be advisable to have the child evaluated by a speech pathologist. The parents should call local public school offices for "Child Find" resources, whose responsiblity it is to locate children with special needs and provide needed therapy.

- Work closely with the family and any special needs professionals when a child is diagnosed with a specific problem. Therapy and techniques should be consistent in the family and the child care situation for best results.

KEEP RECORDS OF CHILDREN'S LANGUAGE DEVELOPMENT

To heighten your awareness of children's progress in speaking, have a language section in the anecdotal records you keep on each child. (See Curriculum chapter.) When you hear a child say something unusual or seem to exhibit progress in speech, write down what the child said and the date. Over time you will see speech unfold in fascinating ways. An additional possibility is to make a short tape recording of a child's language once a month. Have a separate cassette tape for each child. At the end of the last month's speech, record the date and then have a short conversation with the child.

Activities related to language development in *Things to Do with Toddlers and Twos:* pp. 75; 77–78; 99–100

RESOURCES

Books:

Derman-Sparks, Louise, *Anti-bias Curriculum*, NAEYC. 1988. This book contains an excellent reference section of recommended children's books pp. 119–133, to help you locate books featuring a diversity of people.

Jalongo, Mary Renck, *Young Children and Picture Books—Literature from Infancy to Six*. NAEYC, Washington, DC, 1988. Much fine advice on selecting and using books.

Strickland, Dorothy S., and Lesley Mandel Morrow, Editors, *Emerging Literacy: Young Children Learn to Read and Write*. International Reading Association, Newark, Delaware. 1989. The collection of essays in this book give the reader a thorough understanding of the processes involved in learning to read and write—helpful when talking to parents about appropriate activities. Bernice Cullinan gives an excellent discussion of selecting books for children in Chapter 1.

Trelease, Jim, *The Read Aloud Handbook*, 2nd revised edition, Penguin, 1989. This fine resource gives parents and teachers many useful insights on getting children hooked on books, as well as a review of many children's book titles to help you choose good titles.

Video Tape:

Drummond, Tom, *Comments and Conversations: Talk that Teaches*. Available from Media Distribution, North Seattle Community College, 9600 College Way N., Seattle, WA 98103. $275. This is a very useful video tape that shows how teachers can expand on children's language and encourage children to express themselves and communicate effectively. It contains bad examples as well as good examples. Appropriate for older preschool children as well as toddlers and two-year-olds.

CHAPTER 4

Communicating with Music

Since time began, people have communicated with music. Singing and dancing is as natural to toddlers as talking and walking. Your main task is to maintain and build on this natural aptitude. Give children many opportunities to sing and dance. Let them see that these are fun things to do, things they can do together with others. Singing to young children can stimulate listening skills and augment over-all language development. Singing and dancing give children more ways to express themselves which can have emotional benefits as well as language benefits. Remember that children copy the behaviors of adults who are important to them, so sing a lot yourself, and dance "when the spirit moves you." The more you sing, the more your children will sing.

HOW TO GET TODDLERS TO SING

Don't worry about the "quality" of singing, or correct a child's singing. Toddlers will join in on certain phrases and leave out others. Young children will rarely sing on pitch, but their voices will go up and down at appropriate times, according to the melody of a song. As with other forms of creative expression, with singing, it is the process, not the product that is important.

- As well as bursting into spontaneous song throughout the day, try singing as a small group activity when children can pay attention well.
- Start with simple chanting. Don't worry about words. Pick a simple melody, such as "Mary Had a Little Lamb," and sing "la, la, la" instead of words. Add words later.
- Stick to familiar nursery songs. They usually have simple melodies that have withstood the test of time.
- Sing fairly slowly. If you rush through a song, children will not be able to keep up. The idea is not to "perform" for the children, but to have them join in and enjoy the process.
- Sing in a medium pitch. Try to match the average pitch of children's normal speaking voices so their chances of matching the tone are greater.
- Let children learn to experiment with volume. See if they can sing a familiar song very softly and loudly. Discourage shouting, however.
- You could introduce a new song every Monday and add it to your songbook. Send the words home with parents so they can sing along with their child at home and reinforce the new song.

CLASS SONGBOOK

Materials:

Small photo album or	*Hole punch*
looseleaf notebook	*Background paper*
Clear self-adhesive plastic	*Drawing materials*

As you teach children a new song, make a simple illustration of it—a symbol to represent the song, such as a lamb for "Mary Had a Little Lamb." Write down the words to the song as well, for the benefit of other adults. Place this songbook where children

have access to it. You may be surprised to hear phrases of the songs as children flip through the pages by themselves or with a friend. This songbook will help you to remember to repeat songs you have taught children so they don't forget them over time.

MAKE UP YOUR OWN SONGS

Pick any familiar melody, such as "Old MacDonald Had a Farm" or "Twinkle, Twinkle Little Star" and add simple rhyming words that describe events the children have experienced. These may become children's favorite songs. For example:

> *"Jeffrey Johnson has new shoes . . . ee-ei-ee-ei-o.*
> *Jeffrey's brand new shoes are blue . . . ee-ei-ee-ei-o . . .*
> *With a jump jump here, and a jump jump there,*
> *Here a jump, there a jump, everywhere a jump-jump.*
> *Jeffrey Johnson has new shoes . . . ee-ei-ee-ei-o!"*

PLAY "NAME THAT TUNE"

Materials:

Record player and record with many bands of songs on it. (optional)

Either hum or whistle a familiar melody, or play it on an instrument, or play the recording of familiar songs. Tell children to call out the name of the songs when they recognize which one it is. This "auditory discrimination" exercise is good for teaching listening skills.

FAST AND SLOW MOVEMENTS

Teach children some simple movements to do while they sing familiar songs, such as rowing movements to do while they sing, "Row, Row, Row Your Boat." First have them sing and row slowly, and then quickly. This activity brings shrieks of delight from children.

MOOD DANCING

Materials:

Recorded music of different moods and tempos

At first toddlers simply bounce up and down or sway from side to side when they "dance" to music. So play many different types of music and dance along yourself, simply demonstrating different ways to move your arms and body in response to the music. Comment on what you see other children doing as well. This builds their repertoire of body movements. (Physical—Gross Motor)

DISCOTECH DANCING

Materials:

Lively recorded music to dance to
Brightly colored bathroom rug

Place the brightly colored rug in the middle of a "dance area" or circle. Tell children this is the "spotlight." Invite all the children to dance to the music. Call out one child's name, and that child moves to the spotlight rug to continue dancing. Then call out another child's name. The first child moves off the rug, but still continues to dance at the side, and the new child takes her place. Continue until all children have had a chance to dance on the rug. This activity gives children supervised practice at taking turns while enjoying the spotlight. (Social; Self)

POM POM DANCING

Materials:

Pom poms for each child made of crepe paper streamers cut into 8 inch strips and taped together at one end with masking tape.
Lively recorded music

Let children wave and shake the pom poms as they dance to the music. A favorite activity, this is easy to bring out when you feel you need a change of pace during free-play time, or the children need to burn up some excess energy. (Physical)

RHYTHM INSTRUMENTS

At first, give all the children the same type of instrument to play. This "isolates" the sound of the instrument and children become more conscious of what it can do. Let them learn together how to play the instrument loud and soft, fast and slow, and to start and stop on a signal given by you. Paper towel tubes reinforced with self-adhesive paper are good to start with. When a group of children hit these together at the same time, it produces quite an interesting sound.

Activities related to music in Things to Do with Toddlers and Twos: *pp. 21–27; 78–80; 123; 127–131.*

RESOURCES:

Beall, Pamela Conn, and Susan Hagen Nipp, *Wee Sing—Children's Songs and Fingerplays*, Price/Stern/Sloan Publishers, Inc. 1981.

Beall, Pamela Conn, and Susan Hagen Nipp, *Wee Sing and Play—Musical Games and Rhymes for Children*, Price/Stern/Sloan Publishers, Inc. 1982.

These two books contain words to all the simple songs you remember from childhood, but have forgotten the words.

Seeger, Ruth, *American Folk Songs for Children*. Doubleday, 1948.

A classic book, it presents many simple American music games for young children, giving suggestions for using the children's names in the traditional songs.

Warren, Jean, *Piggy Back Songs*. Warren Press. 1986.

Simple, new lyrics are added to very familiar melodies. An ideal resource for someone who cannot read music, but still wants to sing with children.

CHAPTER 5

Getting in Touch with Senses

Activities involving the five senses—touch, sight, smell, hearing and taste—are "feeders" of creativity. Polly McVicker, who wrote the NAEYC publication, *Imagination,* said, "You have to feed the muscles of the imagination." One way to "feed these muscles" is to give children many experiences using their senses. If a child were to spend his entire life in a blank room, he would not learn or have ideas. When a child experiences many different textures, sounds and smells, he will have mental images available to pull together for a rich imaginative life.

SENSE OF SMELL

The sense of smell has powerful connections to imagination. Whenever I smell a certain perfume the image of a favorite aunt is in front of me. What are your own special smells? The smell of drying autumn leaves might put you back to your childhood jumping into piles of leaves. Perhaps you think of your uncle Joe whenever you smell motor oil. Let's give toddlers lots of interesting things to smell, around which to build pleasant memories.

As you give children experiences with the sense of smell, provide the words that go with the smells. Notice smells outside in the yard or when you take short nature walks at different times of the year. Whenever you do simple cooking projects with children or bring in foods for them to taste, be sure to have them smell them first. Play a guessing game before lunch and see if the children can guess what is cooking. Try bringing in something different for the children to smell every day. See how long you can go without repeating yourself.

SMELL BAGS

Materials:

 Net material   *Materials with strong smells*
 Needle and thread

Sew up some small bags of net and fill them with things that have a distinctive aroma, such as orange peels, cinnamon sticks, cloves, cotton dabbed in various cooking extracts such as lemon, peppermint and almond. (Language)

SMELL BOOK

Materials:

 Perfume strips from magazines
 Report binder or looseleaf binder

Magazines and store circulars sometimes have a "smell strip" advertising a new perfume. Collect these and make a book out of them. Punch holes in the pages and add them to a loose-leaf notebook, or put them in a book report cover with a plastic clamp-type binding. The fragrances last a long time and even give your room a nice smell. You can also make your own smell strips by sprinkling powdered gelatin and spices on glue and letting them dry. Put each different smell on a separate page of your book. This book will be a favorite of your toddlers! (Language)

Activities related to the sense of smell in *Things to Do with Toddlers and Twos:* pp. 64, 65.

SENSE OF TOUCH

The whole world is really one massive collage of textures. Children naturally investigate how things feel to the touch as they explore. Activities that emphasize the sense of touch include playdough, sand play, indoor sand/rice/cornmeal play, water play and fingerpainting. These are all thoroughly discussed in *Things to do with Toddlers and Twos.* Here are a few more ideas to have fun with the sense of touch:

A TAPE COLLECTION

Materials:

Numerous different kinds of tape

Toddlers love to feel the sticky texture of tape and things like self-adhesive paper. Why not develop a "tape collection?" Bring in samples of as many different types of tape as you can find: masking tape; transparent tape; cellophane tape; electric tape; duct tape; adhesive tape; BAND-AIDS!. Give each child a small piece to play with. You could also stick different kinds of tape to a plastic surface such as a plexiglass mirror. Or, make a "tape mural" letting children stick different kinds of tape to a large piece of posterboard. Add to it from time to time. As well as exploring textures, they will have good fine-motor practice. (Physical—Fine Motor)

FEELY BAG PAIRS

Materials:

Pairs of objects
Cloth bag or pillow case

Collect pairs of 3 familiar objects, such as hair brushes, shoes, and balls. (The objects should be very different from each other.) Let the children examine each object and talk about it. Then put one of each pair on the table in front of the child, and keep the others out of sight. Put one of the others in a bag and let the child reach in the bag and feel it, but not see it. Let the child feel the objects that are visible on the table in front of him at the same time, and then guess which one is in the bag. (Cognitive.)

CORNSTARCH GOOP

Materials:

> *Cornstarch—1 box*   *Mixing bowl*
> *Water—enough to make a*   *Food coloring (optional)*
>   *gravy-like consistency*

Simply mix a box of cornstarch and water together in a large bowl. This magic substance becomes solid and warm when you pick it up and squeeze it, but turns liquid and runs between your fingers when you loosen your grip. Add food coloring for fun. Easy to clean up, soothing and fun. Children and adults of all ages have fun with this.

OUTSIDE TEXTURES

Make a survey of the textures that are already on your playground. How many do you have? Grass, concrete, sand, chain link? What can you add? Possibilities: a tree stump or log with bark; large, smooth rocks (too heavy to lift); blankets; water; door mats; a small wooden deck; artificial turf; indoor/outdoor carpeting. Create a "texture path" with some of these materials.

Variations of the "Sticky Picture" in *Things to do with Toddlers and Twos:* (The "Sticky Picture" activity is simply to tape a piece of contact paper to the wall, sticky side out, and let children attach various light objects such as feathers, fabric swatches and tissue paper onto the sticky surface.)

NATURE STICKY PICTURE

Materials:

> *Self-adhesive plastic*
> *Light-weight objects from*
>   *nature*

Take children on a short nature walk, even on the playground or a nearby lot. Let them collect small pieces of grass, leaves, seeds and wildflowers, and put them in small paper bags. Back in the room let the children show everyone what they found and talk about it. Then peel off the backing of a large piece of self-adhesive plastic and let children put their objects onto the sticky surface. This can then be taped to the wall at the children's level so they can go over to it and touch the nature things as well as feel the sticky texture of the paper.

STICKY FEET!

Materials:

Large piece of self-adhesive plastic
Masking tape

This is so much fun for toddlers, you'll be tempted to try it yourself. Simply tape a large piece of self-stick adhesive plastic to the floor, sticky side up. Tape all around the edges so it won't buckle. Then invite a child to walk on it with bare feet! You may see some fancy footwork!

STICKY PICTURES IN A THEME SHAPE
Materials:

Self-adhesive plastic
Light-weight paper and materials of appropriate colors

Cut the self-adhesive plastic in the shape of a teddy bear. Then give children a variety of brown things to stick onto it. Adapt for other themes.

Activities related to the sense of touch in *Things to Do with Toddlers and Twos:* pp. 11–19; 30–33; 49–57; 61.

SENSE OF HEARING

The world of sounds is fascinating to toddlers. At a time when they are rapidly developing language skills, they are imitating all different sounds they hear in their environment. Enrich your environment with things that make interesting sounds.

A SOUND GARDEN

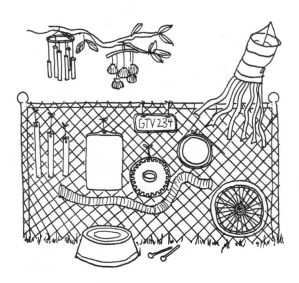

Collect things that make interesting sounds to place in your yard.

Windsocks make lovely noises as they flap in the breeze. Add several wind chimes to give your yard a musical quality. The kind of plastic streamers found at used car lots make a noisy sound and can be fun. Run a wooden stick along your chain link fence. Suspend lengths of metal pipe to hit and make different musical notes. Dangle old hub caps, license plates, pie tins and cookie sheets from a tree or the fence to hit with sticks. How about a long tube to holler through? A galvanized pail or tub makes a great drum. What else can you think of? One program found the "innards" of an old, damaged and discarded piano, and placed that set of strings horizontally on the ground in their yard. Children made wonderful "avant garde" music by hitting the strings with sticks and had fun dancing to it.

A SHAKER COLLECTION

Materials:

> *Cans and unbreakable containers of various shapes and sizes, with lids*
> *Glue, tape*
> *Things to put inside shakers such as rice, stones, salt, cotton balls, walnuts, etc.*

Put a different material inside each container. Glue or tape on the lid securely. Make a collection of these and see how many different ones you can make. Keep them in a large box and present them to two or three children by saying, "Look . . . I have a whole bunch of things in this box that make a noise when you shake them. Which one would you like to try first?" Help the children describe the sounds. You could make pairs of shakers that make the same kind of sound, and see if two-year-olds can find matching pairs. (Language)

Activities related to the sense of hearing in *Things to Do with Toddlers and Twos:* pp. 21–28; 65.

SENSE OF SIGHT

The world is full of fun things to look at!

MIRRORS

Materials:

> *Mirrored plexiglass or mylar*
> *Strong-bonding glue*

It's fun to affix mirrored plexiglass in some of the nooks and crannies of your classroom. Plexiglass can be cut into any shape with a small hand-held electric saw. Look in your Yellow Pages under "plastics" for sources. Another fun possibility is mirrored "mylar," a flexible plastic material available in drafting supply stores. It can be cut with scissors and taped to the wall. It even comes in different colors. Mylar, because it has curves and bumps, gives a distorted reflection which amuses children.

COLORED ACETATE REPORT COVERS
Materials:

Transparent report covers

Transparent plastic sheets used to cover book reports can be found in office supply stores and the school supply section of many variety stores. Toddlers love putting these over their heads and watching the world change colors. Overlapping two different colors shows them a third color.

OUTSIDE SIGHTS

See how you can add some visual excitement to your playground! Possibilities: Hang a crystal and let the children have the thrill of discovering rainbows! Attach panels of colored plexiglass to a chain link fence, where children can look through it and see the world change color. On a sunny day, hang large pieces of bright fabrics for the light to shine through. These could also be used as temporary shade structures. Hang up a wind sock to provide something beautiful to look at as well as rustling sounds in the breeze.

Activities related to the sense of sight in *Things to Do with Toddlers and Twos:* p. 63.

SENSE OF TASTE

Food provides you with the ultimate sensory experience for young children. It is the only type of activity that lets you intentionally use all five senses. It would be good to do at least one food activity a week with children. Of course, also take advantage of the opportunities at regular meal and snack times to talk about how the food looks, sounds, feels, smells and tastes.

Leave complex cooking projects that require measuring, mixing, timing and chemical transformations from baking or chilling to older children. Toddlers live too much in the here and now to get very much out of that type of food experience. Rather than doing elaborate cooking projects with many ingredients such as baking cookies, or making things from mixes where the final product appears like magic, expose toddlers to basic foods and let them explore them like they would any new object. Remember to have children wash hands before they handle food.

EXPLORE AN APPLE

Materials:

Apples   *Plastic picnic knives*

Gather three or four children around a table and show them an apple. They will probably already know what it is and have several things to say about it. Look at all the different colors on it and the little spots. Let them see the stem end and the flower end of the fruit. Let them each twist the stem until it comes off. Then cut the apple in half sideways to expose the star pattern made by the seeds. Let each child smell the cut apple, and touch the white part. Help them notice how the apple is dry on the outside but wet on the inside. Then give each child a small plastic knife. Cut the apple into pieces so each child can have a piece. Let the child use the plastic knife to cut his piece into smaller pieces and eat it. Comment on how an apple makes a "crunch" sound when someone bites off a piece. You might cut a second apple from top to bottom and let children notice the different pattern and shape this produces. This whole process will take about five or ten minutes. But when it is finished, the child is likely to know a lot more about the concept of "apple" than he did before.

FOOD OF THE WEEK

Materials:

Various foods, esp. fruits and vegetables
Camera (optional)

Do the above type activity with other fruits and raw vegetables of all types. You could have a "food of the week," and include it in your lunch or snack menu, prepared in several different ways. Keep a scrapbook with magazine pictures, or even better, photographs of the foods you have explored. Children will enjoy going back over this, and remembering when one of "their" foods appears in their meals. "Oh look. What are these things in the salad? Right, Jessica, they are tomatoes! Remember when we cut up tomatoes? Let's look at the pictures."

BANANAS, HONEY AND WHEAT GERM
Materials:

Bananas	*Wheat Germ*
Honey	*Plastic knives*
Milk	

Here's a simple activity that combines several ingredients. Cut bananas in half and give each child a half to peel. Then let the children cut their banana halves into pieces with a plastic knife. Mix some honey with a little milk to thin it a bit and put it in a small bowl between two children. Put some wheat germ in a second small bowl between them. Let the children dip their banana chunks into the honey first and then into the wheat germ and then pop them into their mouths. Sticky and delicious!

Activities related to the sense of taste in *Things to Do with Toddlers and Twos:* Cooking Projects p. 62.

CHAPTER 6

Art for Creative Toddlers

I was observing in a toddler classroom one time and the teacher told me she was going to have the children make "mailboxes." I silently predicted disaster, but like a good observer, did not interfere. The first red flag was that the teacher had a final product in mind. Children had just come inside from the playground and were playing independently in various parts of the room. She tried to get all twelve children to come to the table at once to do the project. (Red flag number 2.) She sat some of them down at the table, which had nothing on it at that point, and then went to get other children who were engaged elsewhere in the room. In one case there was a protest, the child did not want to leave the doll corner. Another child engaged the teacher in a chase. By the time she got the last two to the table, about five minutes had passed, and three of the children who had been seated had gotten up and wandered away again. One other tipped his chair over and was sitting on it backwards. She then passed out pieces of construction paper and crayons and said to the children, "Today we are making mailboxes. Next week is Valentine's Day, and we will put our Valentines in these boxes, just like the mailman does." (None of this registered with the children.) When the crayons appeared within reach of the toddlers they each grabbed one and made a few scribbles on the paper. The teacher also had a pile of washed out milk cartons and some glue on the table. It had taken her considerable time to collect and wash the cartons, and she spent her last break time trimming the ends. She meant to have the children glue their paper to the cartons. However, as soon as the children had scribbled a few strokes they jumped up from the table and wandered away. She decided to let them go since her assistant could watch them. She hastily printed the name of each child on his paper. She then spent the rest of the play time gluing each paper to the milk cartons herself. She looked at me apologetically and said, "You can't really do art projects with this age group. They don't have the attention span."

What were this teacher's goals? Why did she feel compelled to do this type of project with toddlers? What were her mistakes? How might she have proceeded differently?

SOME GENERAL PRINCIPLES FOR ART WITH TODDLERS

1. Don't tell the children what to make or expect that they will have a recognizable final product. If you tell a two-year-old to make a "mailbox" or an Easter Basket, or draw a doggie, you are setting him up for failure. The child cannot possibly do it himself. Some people have the child color or paint the paper and then do the rest of it themselves, like fashioning a basket. But what does this prove? That the teacher knows how to cut and paste? Instead, value the basic scribble. Worried about what to show the parent? Hand them the scribbled paper and say, "Denise thoroughly enjoyed playing with crayons today. She stayed at this for nearly ten minutes." Children need many experiences freely exploring materials before they will be able to control the materials adequately to make a representational drawing, which will not happen in the toddler years.

2. Focus on providing interesting materials. When toddlers and two-year-olds engage in art projects such as fingerpainting, pasting or painting with a brush, they are basically involved in "exploratory play." They want to see what they can do with the material—how it acts—what it is good for. It is the "cause and effect" action that appeals: action A produces response B. "I move my arm this way and a mark appears on the paper."

The goal of art experiences for this age child is to expose children to many different materials and processes. In painting experiences, for example, let them paint with many different colors of paint, starting with one color at a time. Mix the paint in different ways to make it thick one time, thin another time. Give them many things to paint with over time—short handled brushes from the hardware store about 1 inch wide are good to start with. Then let them use wider and narrower brushes, tooth brushes, shaving brushes, cotton swabs, sponges, pine branches, feathers, etc. Let them paint on many different surfaces, including three-dimensional objects such as boxes and rocks.

3. Let the child do the *whole* project. The more the teacher has to do, the less value the activity has for the children. If you do pasting or gluing activities with children, make sure to let the *children* handle the paste or glue. If the teacher puts the glue on the page for the child, the value of the activity is lost.

4. Do art with one child at a time, or very small groups. Present art projects to the youngest toddlers one at a time. With your undivided attention, the child can really concentrate on the material in front of her and enjoy seeing what she can do with it. Another great advantage of this method of presentation is that it greatly simplifies clean up. You have only one messy pair of hands to wash off at a time.

What about the other children? Have other interesting things in the room for them to be doing. If possible, plan to present art activities at times when there is another adult working with you who can keep an eye on the other children. You may find that some children still prefer to stand around and watch. This is a very common learning style for young toddlers and they are soaking it all in, giving the process a mental rehearsal before it is their turn. As long as they don't crowd the child whose turn it is, and they have the choice of other interesting activities, they should be allowed to choose to watch. A toddler will only maintain interest in an art activity for a few minutes, so turns go quickly.

With two year olds, you can set up an art project so that three or four children can do it at the same time. They will enjoy the "parallel play" aspect of the experience and may even pick up ideas watching other children.

Do avoid sitting the whole group down at once to do an art activity. Inevitably this leads to too much waiting for the children, and they will learn to dislike such activities. Besides, they will all *finish* at the same time which can lead to a crowd at the sink and handprints on the furniture and walls.

5. Allow children to repeat experiences. One of the sweetest questions a teacher can ask a child is, "Do you want to do it again?" This can be a rare phrase in an early childhood setting where the teacher is concerned that every child gets a turn at the activity, so everyone can take something home. Far better to repeat the activity for several days so that each child can fully explore it. If a child can make four or five paintings in a row, it gives him a chance to "work through" the process and learn what happens when paint is applied in different ways. This approach encourages the development of concentration and experimentation, both elements of creativity. Insisting that children can only do one of whatever the activity is encourages a "once over lightly" attitude, and the child does not learn or develop as much.

SCRIBBLING ACTIVITIES

Give children many different materials with which to make lines and scribble. Crayons, regular pencils, colored pencils, wide and narrow felt tipped markers, ball point pens, can all be used with adult supervision. Find different kinds of paper for them to scribble on to vary the experience. DO NOT GIVE CHILDREN COLORING BOOKS OR PATTERNS TO COLOR. Instead, just give them different kinds of plain paper to color on as the year progresses.

VARIATION ON SCRIBBLE EASEL— A FRIENDSHIP EASEL

Materials:

Wide easel   *Yarn*
Fat crayons   *Paper*

Use a wide easel for your scribble easel, attaching several crayons with yarn to the top. Two or more children can scribble on the paper you attach to the easel at the same time, adding an enjoyable "parallel play" aspect to the activity.

MARKERS ON PAPER TOWELS

Materials:

White paper towels
Water based felt-tipped markers (wide point)

Let children make marks on the paper towels with the markers. The lines will widen and blur. Supervise this activity closely so children do not put marker caps in their mouth or suck on the markers. This is a good "spur of the moment–time filler" activity and is enjoyable for the children because it gives them an immediate effect in the streak of bright color.

PAINTING ACTIVITIES

It's wonderfully exciting for a toddler to see a broad streak of bright color appear on a piece of paper when he moves his arm a certain way. Although painting can be messy, it is worth it to "gear up" and offer it to children frequently.

CUP FOR CLEANING UP FINGERPAINT ON THE TABLE TOP

Materials:

> *Paper or styrofoam cup*
> *Fingerpaint or shaving*
>   *cream*

Allow the children to fingerpaint directly on a table top, either with fingerpaint or shaving cream. When they have done this to their hearts' content, give them the cup. Invert the cup and show them how to push it along the table surface. The paint will pile up on the side of the cup, and a nifty "negative space" trail where there is no paint will appear on the table top. Children will enjoy this part of the activity as much as the actual fingerpainting, and your clean-up will be greatly simplified! (Cognitive.)

TALCUM POWDER IN PAINT

Materials:

Tempera paint   *Paper*
Talcum powder (baby   *Brushes*
*   powder)*

Mix talcum powder in with your tempera paint to add a pleasant smell and extend the paint. You will find it adds a glisten and a lovely smooth texture.

HOUSE PAINTER

Materials:

Brushes of different types, such as house painting brushes (small), easel brushes, sponges

Small bucket
Water

Painting with just plain water is great fun for toddlers. On a warm, sunny day put a few inches of water in a bucket and let your children paint the outside of your building with it. Let them try the different sizes of brushes. The toddlers will explore many different surfaces and enjoy seeing the deeper color of the wet surfaces.

FUNNY PAINTING

Materials:

Sunday comics (colored   *Brushes*
*   cartoon pages)*   *Water*
Easel

Attach a page of your Sunday "funnies" paper to the easel and let a child paint it with water. The colors will blur. The child might also recognize some of the characters.

PRINT MAKING ACTIVITIES

Making prints involves pressing an object into some paint and then placing that same object on a piece of paper and lifting it off again. A wonderful art experience for older children, it often falls short with children under three. Often the child simply "scrubs" with the object meant to make the print, really using it as a painting or coloring object. But you might decide that is okay. With a small amount of low-pressure modelling from the adult, the child might be able to learn to press the object onto the paper and lift it off again. In fact, once they get the hang of it, toddlers love to "pound" an object on a piece of paper again and again, making a repeated, overlapping design in the process.

TO MAKE A PRINTING PAD

Materials:

> *A thin sponge cloth or sheet of foam rubber*
> *Styrofoam meat tray*
> *Tempera paint*

Place the sponge or foam rubber in the meat tray and saturate it with tempera paint. Then let the child press the object onto the sponge and then onto paper to make a print.

OBJECTS TO MAKE INTERESTING PRINTS

The process of making prints might make children more aware of all sides of three-dimensional objects. A big flat jar lid makes a big, hollow circle with one side, but a big filled-in circle with the other side. A big, round balloon makes a small round print. See how many different objects you can offer children over time. Some possibilities: cotton swabs; jar lids; corks; golf balls; sponges; apples; green peppers; odd puzzle pieces; blocks of different shapes; film canisters; cookie cutters; fit-together toys; sneaker soles; tomato baskets. Later see if children can remember what object made which print.

COMMERCIAL RUBBER STAMPS

Rubber stamps have recently become available in a wide variety of child-oriented designs. Children can use them with a commercial printing stamp, or they can color on the surface of the stamp with water-based felt markers (supervise), and then press the stamp onto paper. The markers are fun because the child can later wipe the stamp with a damp cloth or sponge and use a different color marker to change the color of the design. Relatively non-messy, this is a good end of the day activity.

PASTING AND GLUING ACTIVITIES

Young children love to make things stick. It is the mechanical process that fascinates them—the magic of it. Let the children experiment with a variety of different ways to make things stick, including homemade paste, school paste, white glue and various kinds of tape. You will notice that the children are as interested in the sticky substance on their hands as they are in the arrangement on the paper. The idea is to let children experiment with many different materials over time. So make three collections:

1. Different materials to make things stick: white glue; school paste; homemade flour and water paste; glue stick; masking tape; cellophane tape; transparent tape.
2. Interesting materials to stick down: tissue paper; construction paper scraps; small fabric scraps of different textures; feathers; leaves; pine needles; old greeting cards; dry pasta shapes; yarn; etc.
3. Surfaces to serve as a "base" on which to stick things: construction paper; cardboard; paper plates; index cards; shoebox lids; egg cartons; etc.

Concentrate on giving children an ever-changing variety of the above materials, adding variety to the same basic activity. Be sure to allow the child to do the *whole* project. Do not put the glue on the paper for her. Toddlers are often more fascinated with watching the glue come out of the bottle than they are with spreading it on the paper and could conceivably use up your whole bottle of glue in one sitting. Instead of giving the toddler the bottle to squeeze, pour a small amount of glue into a jar lid or small dish and give her a cotton swab or other implement to use as a spreader.

Activities related to art in *Things to Do with Toddlers and Twos:* pp. 29–47.

RESOURCES:

Cherry, Clare, *Creative Art for the Developing Child,* Fearon
   Teachers' Aids, 1990.
   The "classic" art book of our field, it explores all the different
   processes and how children benefit.

CHAPTER 7

Let's Pretend!

    Adults can first glimpse the imagination of a child when her play takes on a "Let's pretend!" quality. Dramatic play is one of the most valuable forms of play in childhood. Besides being an outlet for the child's imagination, it helps her develop social skills and understandings, deal with emotional issues, develop vocabulary and expressive language skills and also develop cognitive understandings, especially in using symbols to represent real things.

COGNITIVE BENEFITS OF DRAMATIC PLAY

In a sense, it is its cognitive value that is the most exciting thing about dramatic play, especially when we see it in our youngest children. It is in dramatic play that we see a child's first use of *symbols* . . . things that represent something else. Just as the written word, *telephone*, represents something else, a real telephone,—a toy telephone also represents something else from what it is—it also represents a real telephone. The child *knows* that the toy telephone is not real. The child is using the toy to *represent* the real thing. What this tells us is that the child is able to retain a *mental image* of an object that is not right there.

Symbolic Thinking in Dramatic Play

Realistic objects.   At first toddlers use objects that are very realistic to represent something real. A toy telephone, pots and pans and play dishes, steering wheels, toy cars, and shopping carts are popular props with toddlers.

Improvised props. Later, when the child has had more experience with this type of play, she becomes more skillful in *improvising* props. When a child takes a round paper plate and pretends it is a steering wheel, or lifts a block to her ear, her use of symbols is even more apparent to us.

Gestures and actions. Eventually, the child may use hand gestures or positions to indicate an imaginary prop that isn't there at all. Simply holding the hand to the ear to represent a telephone, moving hands in front of herself to represent a non-existent steering wheel, or lifting a pretend cup are examples.

Bridge to Reading and Mathematics

Letters and words are symbols. When children use pretend objects to represent real objects, it becomes easier for them to understand, later, that little black marks on a piece of paper (letters) could represent sounds that represent objects. Likewise, it can become easier to comprehend that other little black marks (numerals) can represent quantities of objects.

Sequencing. When the child plays out a simple plot, she demonstrates the understanding that events must happen in a certain order to make sense. First you put the dishes on the table, then you pour the coffee, then you and your guests drink the coffee, then you wash the dishes. When a child has acted out a plot of her own making, it becomes easier for her to follow the events in a story.

Learning the Difference Between Fantasy and Reality

Very young children have difficulty knowing what is real and what is pretend. That is why costumed characters sometimes frighten them. The more experience they have with dramatic play, the easier it becomes for them to sort it out and know what "pretend" means. In fact, older two-year-olds will sometimes announce, "This is just pretend." Related to this is learning the difference between thoughts and wishes and real things.

OTHER VALUES OF DRAMATIC PLAY

Developing the Sense of Self

When a child imitates important adults in his life, it is like saying, "I can do that too." The child establishes his position as a fellow human being. When he becomes aware of the wider variety of roles people play, he develops a stronger sense of where he fits in, and what the options and possibilities are.

Imagination and Creativity

Through dramatic play, a child learns that she can make things happen in her own world—that she has the power to set the scene and control the action. If adults remain non-judgmental and non-controlling, the child is free to explore all kinds of situations, and know that her mind has the power to create, change, and "un-do" things. In later years this will show up in representational art work, story writing and other forms of creativity.

Developing Empathy

Through dramatic play the child becomes more aware of other people and their roles. The child must closely observe the actions of other people to imitate them in play later. When he has had many experiences playing other roles, it becomes easier for him to *empathize* with other people—to understand and have sympathy for how they are feeling. It is, literally, the ability to "put yourself in someone else's shoes."

Developing Social Skills

Dramatic play with other children also develops a child's social play skills. The child must learn how to enter the play, how to fit in with the action, how to copy ideas and add ideas. At first she will be an imitator of others, performing the same actions as the other children. Later she might take on the "leader" role, being the one to initiate actions that others will imitate.

Emotional Values

Sometimes children will act out things that are frightening to them in real life. Going to the doctor, for instance, is a favorite play theme. When the child recreates scary situations, he puts himself in charge and gains a feeling of control. He knows he can stop the action, change the situation or drop out of the play at any time, if it gets too scary. Pretend situations allow the child to "try on" behaviors in a non-threatening place.

Language

The child often uses dramatic play situations of his own making to "try out" words and phrases he has heard. When a child plays with other people, he not only talks from *within* the role, he talks *about* the role. There must be some basic understanding of what you are playing. In fact, dramatic play skill and activity often increase greatly as the child gains the ability to understand others and be understood. Dramatic play is a fine *motivator* for using language effectively. The child learns that language is power— the power to get people to act in a certain way.

TWO TYPES OF PRETEND PLAY

There are two different styles of pretend play that children engage in. One is when the child actually takes on a role and pretends to be someone, possibly involving dress-up clothes or props to "transform" himself. This is the most common form of pretend play for younger children. It is more direct and more flexible. The advantage is that it can happen anywhere, whether or not there are toys available.

The other type of play is when children manipulate miniature people and animals and vehicles, controlling the action and speaking for the various characters. The child takes on the role of an all-powerful giant who can make things happen and control the scene. This play usually involves toys such as miniature vehicles, small plastic people, doll houses and furniture, blocks, and/or commercial "play scenes" such as garages or airports.

Both types of play have similar benefits to children. Either type can be played by the child as a solitary player or with other children or adults. Both can be highly imaginative, and involve use of symbols as well as language.

LEVELS OF DRAMATIC PLAY

Just as with other developmental behaviors, pretend play moves from the simple to the complex with experience. A child's level of play is not necessarily predictable by her age. Rather, it is the child's developmental stage, language ability, and also important, amount of experience that matters. A child whose parents or older siblings have long engaged her in pretend play will likely be performing at a more complex level than a child who has been left to her own devices.

- *Children imitate what they have seen.* This is the first form of pretend play and it usually starts around the child's first birthday. A child copies a gesture of an adult—standing with hands on hips, pretending to talk on the telephone, or pretending to read a book to a doll for example. The child is not yet really taking on a role, but simply copying things she has seen adults do, without fully understanding them. One year olds are more likely to be imitators than pretenders. Follow the leader games or, "Can you do what I do?" games are ways to build on children's abilities to imitate.

- *Children take on a role.* Soon you will see children pretend to be someone else. Often a prop, such as a hat, helps the transformation. A purse over the arm suddenly transforms a little girl into "Mommy." You will see her act out simple routines familiar to her, such as putting a baby to bed, washing a baby, setting the table and cooking dinner, driving a car, etc. Gradually the child moves from familiar roles and simple sequences to roles of people outside of the family and more complex plots. The complexity of the plot can be greatly influenced by an adult playmate.

- *The child uses props for play.* At first the props must be quite realistic—an obvious representation of a real object. Gradually the child becomes able to use more abstract objects or even simply gestures with no object. All of this is possible with experienced two-year-olds. Often, especially with younger children, the play is prompted by an interesting looking prop—the child sees it and instantly uses the prop. Later he learns to *plan* the play and gather the props he needs ahead of time.

- *Language is incorporated into play.* In fact, dramatic play skills make a quantum leap when the child has a good use of language as he approaches three years of age. The child may start to talk for a doll as well as say things himself. The child also speaks from *within* the role, saying things the *doctor* (or whatever role is being played) would say, not what a little boy would likely say.

WHAT LIES AHEAD?

Older children engage in more complex play themes. Rather than repeatedly acting out familiar scenes, older children act out scary events, or take flights into fantasy themes such as space travel, slaying dinosaurs, or engaging in superhero play. (When a two-year-old engages in superhero play it is usually simply imitation of what he has seen older children do.)

Older children are much more likely to take on a variety of different roles and interact with each other from within their roles. Twos can begin to do this with adults gently pulling them along, but in play with other children they usually either imitate what the other children are doing or take orders from the older children.

TEN WAYS FOR ADULTS TO ENHANCE THE VALUE OF DRAMATIC PLAY FOR TODDLERS AND TWO-YEAR-OLDS

1. *Value this type of play.* Allow it. Encourage it. Learn to recognize it. Observe it. Take notes about what the children are doing and keep a record.

2. *Allow time for dramatic play.* Make sure there is plenty of unstructured play time in your day for children to invent their own play, time when adults are not telling children what to do or leading them in activities.

3. *Provide space and basic equipment.* It is good to have a corner of the room sectioned off for dramatic play, although certainly allow pretend play to go on in other places as well.

4. *Encourage dramatic play outside.* Your outdoor environment can be a prime setting for dramatic play. Children can range farther and be louder and more active than indoors. There is the wonderful added element of riding toys! A climber has numerous possibilities.

5. *Provide dress-up clothes.* Find simple things the child can put on himself, such as large T-shirts that can be pulled over the head, vests and jackets. Enlarge button holes and buttons, or substitute velcro for difficult fasteners. Scarves, jewelry and sunglasses with unbreakable lenses are popular.

6. *Provide "props" for play.* Provide objects children can use, such as lunch boxes, shopping bags, dishes, pots and pans, keys, a toy telephone, etc. New props will inspire new play. Add a cash register or a steering wheel and watch what happens. Unlike older children, two-year-olds are not likely to ask you for certain things they can use as props. But notice what they seem to be playing and subtly add something that will help them carry out the theme. One caution: Too many props can distract children from dramatic play. They end up simply rearranging and manipulating the props as ends in themselves. Children don't need to have absolutely everything possible to go along with a play theme—just a few key objects to spark the ideas.

7. *Provide small toys* for the type of play in which the child becomes the controlling giant—small people and animals, blocks, toy vehicles, playscapes, ramps, doll houses, toy villages, miniature railroads, etc. Also add abstract things like carpet samples, pieces of pvc pipe or cardboard cylinders and spray can tops to augment the scenes. Create interesting places to drive small vehicles—platforms, ledges, tunnels, ramps, etc. Add blocks to the sand area. Your playground sand area can be a prime area for dramatic play. Collect some old wooden unit blocks, or any sanded pieces of wood and add them to the sand toys. Children can push them to make roads, use them as pretend vehicles and stand them upright in the sand. Together with plastic people and animals, they provide materials for dramatic play as well as construction.

8. *Provide experiences.* Young children can only act out experiences they have witnessed themselves , , , adding their own interpretation. This is especially true of toddlers and two-year-olds who cannot gain "second hand" experiences from language (being told about them) as well as older children. Don't expect children to play circus, for example, if they have never seen a circus. If you can take simple field trips—to a laundromat or a grocery store, for example—these experiences will be reenacted with great enthusiasm in the classroom. See what props you can devise to reflect the experience.

9. *Play along.* Left to their own devices, toddlers and two-year-olds act out roles in a rather limited way, often repeating the same actions over and over again. A parent or caregiver

can play along, expanding the role by making suggestions, using props, modeling new behaviors, or adding language, but be careful not to dominate the play.

- Observe before you join in. If the child seems deeply involved, your participation is probably not necessary.
- Ask permission to join the play, unless, of course, you are invited. If the child doesn't want a playmate just then, respect her wishes.
- As much as possible, take your lead from the child. Make your actions fit what she is already doing. If she is playing store, show up as a customer, for instance, but if the child is playing doctor, you could arrive with a bad tummy ache.
- Talk to the child's *role* from within your role. "Oh, Doctor, my baby is sick. Can you make her feel better?" "Mrs. Storekeeper, do you have any macaroni and cheese. It's my child's favorite thing to eat." Extend the child's response. "Is there anything else I can do?" "How much do I owe you?"
- Talk for dolls and stuffed animals, showing children how to give them voices, personalities and feelings.
- Model interesting things to do. "Parallel play" beside the child playing with vehicles, for instance, and build a ramp to make the cars go down, or a garage. Invite her to park her cars in your garage. Help her think of other interesting props to add or things to do.

10. *Simply be an appreciative audience for the child's play.* Sit back and enjoy the show. Let parents in on the fun! Use this chapter to tell parents how important this kind of play is. Encourage them to play with their child at home and enjoy being a kid again. Marvel at what can come from inside the child!

Activities related to dramatic play in *Things to Do with Toddlers and Twos:* pp. 67–74.

RESOURCES

Segal, Marilyn and Don Adcock, *Just Pretending—Ways to Help Children Grow Through Imaginative Play*, Prentice Hall. 1981. Many useful insights and ideas.

CHAPTER 8

Get Ready, Get Set, Go!

It is with great adventure and pride that children learn new physical skills. Picture the face of a child who has just taken her first step, or climbed to the top of the climber for the first time. Gross motor activity, using the large muscles of the legs, arms and torso, and balance and coordination, is the most noticeable thing about toddlers and two-year-olds. Children are discovering the possibilities and limitations of their own bodies. They are "on-the-go" almost all the time! You've probably heard about the study in which an athlete was told to imitate exactly the actions of a toddler for an hour. This prime athlete was totally exhausted in a very short time and couldn't keep up with the toddler! Try it yourself!

Toddlers are very busy learning about the space that surrounds them—where they will fit, what is behind things, what will go through what, etc. Through the use of their bodies in feeling and exploring spaces, they are learning to interpret what their senses tell them.

A new walker holds her arms out for balance and has a very wide-legged stance. As the toddler gains experience, she needs arms for balance less and is very fond of carrying things around in her arms. The stiff, choppy gait of a toddler gradually smooths out into the fluid, arm swinging walk of two-year-olds. The child also busily experiments with other fun ways to move. Running, throwing, jumping, climbing are pursued with vigor.

Since their skill in moving is often greater than their judgment, close supervision is necessary. Take a look at the "Safety" chapter to make sure your environment does not have unnecessary hazards. Remember that the most important safety feature is attentive adults. Be there to protect, and encourage and allow.

Adults do not *teach* children physical skills. A child simply will not learn to do something before he is physically ready. You cannot teach a child to grow taller. Neither can you teach a child to balance on one foot, to climb up a climber, or to walk down stairs with alternating feet before the muscles and nerves have matured properly to do so.

What we *can* do is give children many opportunities to practice the new physical skills that are showing up. This means giving children an environment that is safe to explore, so we are not constantly putting limits on them. It also means providing many interesting materials and activities that allow them to use their muscles in the new ways they have recently mastered. You do not have to encourage children to practice. They do it naturally and compulsively.

Enjoy the magic of it—the wonder of it. Watch the unfolding show!

GROSS MOTOR ACTIVITIES

Walking, Running and Carrying

A WALKING TRAIL

Materials:

Colored self-adhesive paper
Scissors

Cut out numerous footprints (both left feet and right feet) and affix them to the floor, spacing to fit a toddler's stride, to make a trail that goes in interesting directions. Children will enjoy trying to walk along it, putting their feet in the footprints. Variation: see if they can follow each other's footprints in the snow.

LET'S SNEAK!

Toddlers enjoy exploring different ways to move, including walking on tip toe. Challenge the children to see how quietly they can tip toe down the hall and back.

RUNNING AFTER BUBBLES

Materials:

Small, safe electric fan (spaces too small for fingers)
Bubble solution

Turn on the fan and blow bubbles in front of it. The children will greatly enjoy chasing the bubbles into the room and stomping on them. (You can also do this without the fan.) Put the fan away when you are finished with the activity. Great fun on a windy day outside. As children run, aiming for bubbles, they are gaining practice in controlling the direction of their running and in making quick turns and stops.

I'M GONNA GET YOU!

This has been the favorite toddler game since the beginning of time. No instruction necessary—just get down on all fours and say slowly, "I'm gonna get you. . . ." Play this game outside where there is plenty of room because that phrase will be followed by shrieks of delighted laughter and wild running as you pretend to chase children. It's even better if you have something to run around such as a tree or a shed. One caution—play this game only after children know you well and trust you!

LARGE, LIGHT OBJECTS TO LIFT AND CARRY

Children this age like to feel big and powerful, and carrying big objects helps them feel this way. Large inflatable beach toys can serve this purpose well, and they can be deflated and put away again.

CONTAINERS WITH HANDLES COLLECTION

We know that toddlers love containers with handles—things like purses, shopping bags, baskets and buckets, carts and wagons. Maybe it is because they have a fascination with moving stuff around. One teacher had a "shopping bag collection" which she hung on the peg-board back of a shelf. The collection grew all year. Children loved filling the bags with small toys and carrying them all over the room. As well as the activity of filling and emptying things, children may be engaging in dramatic play.

DROPPING OBJECTS FROM HEIGHTS
Materials:

Basket with a handle
Small, soft toys such as bean bags, sponges, fabric balls and stuffed animals
Climber or staircase

Let the child fill the basket with the soft toys and carry the basket up stairs (your outdoor climber, perhaps) and then drop the objects over the edge and watch them fall. If you wish, place a clothes basket underneath to catch the objects. Then have the child take the basket back down, fill it again, and repeat the activity as long as it is fun.

TEAR IT UP

Materials:

Newspaper

This is a good group activity when weather prevents you from going outside. Get a stack of newspaper and let children discover all the ways they can make a noise with it. Spread some on the floor and let children step up and down on it together. Crumple some, then invite the children to tear it up into smaller and smaller pieces. It is a satisfying experience for children and makes an interesting noise when many people are tearing at the same time. Then, of course, let children go on a search for every little scrap of paper and put them all in a large laundry basket, so the room is clean again.

Throwing Objects and Playing with Balls

When you think about it, throwing is quite an amazing skill. The child must learn to hold onto an object, move her arm in just the right way, and let go of the object at just the right time to see it go sailing through the air. No wonder it is such a fascination for toddlers! Young toddlers aren't very good at throwing. At most, they kind of "flip" something. Two-year-olds, on the other hand, get pretty good at throwing things.

True, throwing is often a "problem behavior," when children throw objects and endanger other children or windows. The best solution is to devise legitimate throwing activities, indoors and outdoors.

STOCKING BALLS

Materials:

Old pantyhose (support hose work best)
Fabric dye of several colors (optional)
Polyester fiberfill stuffing

Cut the legs off the pantyhose and discard the tops. Dye the hose different colors according to package directions on the fabric dye box (optional). Tie a knot at the bottom of one of the legs. Cut the fabric directly below the knot. Then stuff a handful or two of polyester stuffing material in the leg over the knot. Tie another knot over the stuffing and cut the fabric directly above the second knot. You have a great soft ball, perfect for throwing indoors or out, because it will not hurt or break anything. You can probably get three balls from each leg. The more you have the better! Toss these balls in the washing machine and dry them in the dryer when they get dirty.

THROW THE BALLS INTO THE CORNER

Materials:

> A large number of stocking balls (above)—20 or 30.
> Laundry basket (or large box)

Use furniture to block off one corner of the room. Place the laundry basket full of stocking balls in the opposite corner of the room. Challenge the children to throw all of the balls from the laundry basket into the corner you have blocked off. It will take them several tries. Then, with the children, look around to check and see that all of the balls have made it into the corner. When they agree that this is the case, put all of the children in that corner and have them throw the balls back into the laundry basket in another corner! Continue this as long as there is interest. This is a great activity to do indoors on a rainy day when children need to get rid of extra energy.

THROW AT A TARGET

Materials:

> Bean bags, balls, stocking balls or other soft things to throw
>   (the more the better)
> Wading pool

A child's portable plastic wading pool is a great "first target" into which to throw things! Set the pool in a part of the playground where toys won't accidentally be thrown over a fence. Bring out a large box of things to throw. Invite the children to take things from the box and throw them into the wading pool, then back into the box.

BALL COLLECTION

Make a collection of as many different kinds of balls as you can find for your toddlers to play with. Include rubber playground balls of several sizes, ping pong balls, tennis balls, a football, a wiffle ball and a large beach ball. (Don't include balls smaller than ping pong balls, such as jacks balls, because children could choke on these.) Children will have great fun playing with these balls and learning about their different properties.

POP BOTTLE BOWLING

Materials:

Several empty plastic liter pop bottles
Balls of several sizes

Show the children how to stand a few empty plastic pop bottles upright on the floor and then roll a ball toward them from several feet away and try to knock them down. The child can set them up again himself and try again and again. Keep it light and non-competitive. Let the child decide where to stand, which ball to use and how to set up the bottles. Also consider adding other materials to knock over such as boxes and stuffed animals.

PUSHING BALLS THROUGH A TUNNEL

Materials:

A short tunnel, such as one that comes with a climber, or cardboard storage barrel (clean), or cardboard boxes with the ends removed, taped end to end.
Balls (as many as you have)
Table or platform

Place the tunnel on the table or platform. Give the child a box with lots of balls. Let the child stand at one end of the tunnel and push the balls through the tunnel so they roll out the other end. Another child could catch the balls coming through. Try with toy vehicles.

PUNCHING BALL ON SLINKY

Materials:

Punching ball or beach ball
Plastic "Slinky" toy
Paper towel tubes (optional)

Attach one end of the Slinky to the ceiling. Attach the ball to the other end so it hangs about four feet off the ground. Let the children hit the ball with their hand or with a paper towel tube. The ball will bounce up and down as well as back and forth. The child gains practice with balance as she swings her arms to hit something over her head. (The ball or other soft object, such as a stuffed toy, could simply be hung with string.)

Climbing

Toddlers are such compulsive climbers, it is really advisable to have some sturdy commercially made climbing apparatus designed for toddlers inside as well as outside. This allows you to redirect the activity to a safe place if the child is climbing on something inappropriate, such as a bookshelf. Make sure there is a soft surface such as a mat under the climber to cushion any falls. In a home environment, children love to climb on furniture. You will have to decide what is safe and what you will allow.

STAIRS

Stairs are endlessly enticing to young toddlers. You could easily spend a lovely morning going up and down a flight of stairs with one or two children at a time if your energy matched theirs. Teach them how to go down stairs backwards on their tummies. If possible, carpet stairs thickly. Fence off stairs with a gate when you are not there to supervise closely. A small set of steps in your room will get much use. It is typical for children to walk up and down stairs putting both feet on each step at this age. Don't worry about teaching children to alternate feet going up and down stairs. That will come naturally with maturation.

Riding Toys

Toddlers greatly enjoy propelling a wheeled toy, pushing feet against the floor. They are learning how to steer, and they are also learning how to use their bodies to make something go and stop.

A GARAGE FOR RIDING TOYS

Materials:

Large cardboard box, such as appliance box
Paint

Place the large box on its side and remove one side. Paint lines for "parking spaces" on the "floor" inside the box. Children will enjoy riding their wheel toys inside the box and backing them out again.

RIDING TOY ROAD

Materials:

Chalk or paint, or tape for inside.

If you have a large "patio" area outside for riding toys, consider painting parallel lines to make a road. Or inside, the road could be made by sticking tape on the floor in two parallel lines. See if the child can "drive" the toy within the lines. Make it fun by making the road go in interesting directions, around curves, behind objects, etc. Inside, this might help to contain the riding toys in one particular area. (You could also block off part of the room with furniture.)

RIDING TOY TUNNEL

Materials:

Large appliance box, or sheet and ropes . . . use your ingenuity.

See if you can create a tunnel for children to ride wheel toys through for extra fun and adventure. Maybe you could take the ends off a large appliance box and place the box on its side, bracing it so it does not collapse, and let the children ride through. Or, string up some clothesline and drape a blanket or sheet over it. Besides having fun, children might absorb the concepts of "under" and "through."

Learning to Use a Tricycle

Older twos can begin exploring a tricycle, although it will be difficult for most. They start by simply pushing their feet against the ground rather than the pedals. When they discover the pedals, they are not sure when each foot should be pressed down, and they find out it takes more force to start than to keep going. They might even go backward instead of forward. But what exhilaration when they discover how to make the contraption work! It's probably as big a thrill as when you learned to ride a two-wheel bike later . . . remember? Make sure tricycle is right size so the child can reach the pedals.

Activities related to gross motor development in *Things to Do with Toddlers and Twos:* pp. 117–132.

RESOURCES

Video Tape:

Gerber, Magda, *See How They Move*, Resources for Infant Educarers, 1550 Murray Circle, Los Angeles, CA. 20006. $85.
This exquisite video tape celebrates the beauty of gross motor development of infants and toddlers and makes a strong point about not pushing children to do things before the ability emerges naturally.

CHAPTER 9

Mastering the
Mechanics of Life

The term, "fine motor" refers mainly to a person's ability to use his hands in coordinated ways. For adults it can determine the ability to operate machinery, play musical instruments and do precision work. For the school child it is learning to use writing implements. A preschool child is eagerly learning to operate the fasteners of clothing, put together puzzles and enjoy art materials. Toddlers are busy learning to feed themselves, take *off* clothing, make marks, combine things and stick them together, open and close things and, in general, master the basic mechanics of living.

It is with great seriousness and concentration that a toddler pursues new fine motor skills. The activities take on the level of a compulsion, with the child performing an action over and over again. Watch the concentration on the face of the child who pokes the stiffened end of a shoelace through the hole of a large wooden bead. The toddler's time is spent busily filling and emptying containers, tearing paper, unbuttoning buttons, unscrewing knobs from cabinets, opening lids, sticking things in holes, pounding, rolling and pulling playdough, and picking up small objects. To support a child's growing fine motor skill development, give him many safe and interesting objects to manipulate.

ACTIVITIES FOR FINE MOTOR DEVELOPMENT

When infants start to pick things up, they use a "raking" motion with their hands . . . all their fingers work in unison. Then toward the end of the first year, they begin to use thumb and forefinger together in a "pincer" motion. Toddlers are still refining this skill as well as elegant "poking" motions using one finger at a time.

POKE BOX

Materials:

*Shallow box, such as
    handkerchief or stocking
    box
Contact paper
Small pieces of materials of
    interesting textures such
    as: fake fur, net, felt,
    sandpaper, satin and
    velvet.
Glue, scissors*

*In the lid of the box, cut 6 holes
(or as many as the number of textures you have) about ½ inch in
diameter. On the inside of the box,
lined up under the holes, glue the texture pieces. Place the lid
on the box, and cover the whole thing with contact paper. Cut
the paper from the middle of the holes out to the edge and fold
under. The child will enjoy sticking a finger through the holes to
feel the texture underneath. This activity gives children practice
using one finger independently of the rest. (Creative—Sensory;
Language)*

FINGER PUPPETS

Materials:

*Old cotton or rubber glove
Scissors
Marking pens*

*Cut off the fingers of an old glove to make
simple finger puppets for children. Use
marking pens to draw on faces. You can
also add other details with scraps of fabric,
yarn and fake fur.*

TEAR AND PASTE

Materials:

Junk mail, old wrapping   Paste
*   paper   Paper*

*Collect junk mail, old wrapping paper, or any other paper you
are planning to throw out anyway. Invite a child to tear it up
into many small pieces. Then let the child paste the pieces onto
a paper bag or other piece of paper. Use school paste, or make
some simple paste from flour and water. This activity exercises
a child's "pincer" muscles of thumb and forefinger—muscles that
will be used later in writing. (Creative—Art)*

SQUISH BAGS

Materials:

Sandwich size zip closure   Shaving cream
*   plastic bags   Food coloring*

*With your help, let the child press the button on the shaving cream
can to put some shaving cream inside of the bag. Then let the
child pick out two different colors of food coloring and put a squirt
of each in with the shaving cream. Close the zip closure for the
child. Then let her squeeze the bag to mix the colors. While gaining*

*some good fine-motor practice squeezing the bag, the child will
also enjoy the surprise of seeing two colors mix to make a third
color, a beautiful pastel. This is a good activity to relieve tension
as well. (Creative: Language.)*

SPONGE TRANSFER

Materials:

    Sponges   *Water*
    Two large bowls or dishpans

*Children are fascinated by sponges. Place two dish pans or large
bowls next to each other and put a little water in one. (You could
add a touch of food coloring just for fun.) Then let the child use
the sponges to transfer the water from one tub to the other and
back again. See if you can collect several types of sponges to
make this activity even more interesting.*

SAND BOX FUN

Materials:

    *Wide variety of containers such as food storage containers, both
        square and round, plastic panty hose eggs, measuring cups,
        plastic bottles, funnels, pie tins, etc.*
    Large spoons and plastic shovels to dig with.

Make maximum use of your sandbox. Children love to fill containers with sand and pour them out again. Notice that filling things is not as easy for children as we might imagine. They have to rotate their wrists to make the sand pour out of the shovel at the right time, and often the sand misses the container. When children pour sand from one container to another they are also learning about size and quantity. To keep interest high, change the containers from time to time. (Cognitive)

COTTON BALL TRANSFER

Materials:

> *Cotton balls*
> *Spoon*
> *2 bowls or boxes*

Place all the cotton balls in one bowl. Let the child use the spoon to transfer one cotton ball at a time to the other bowl. He must rotate his wrist to make the cotton ball fall off the spoon into the bowl.

THINGS WITH LIDS COLLECTION

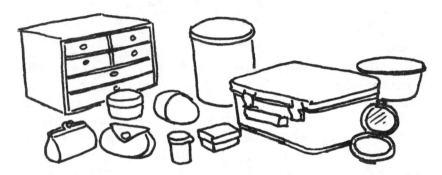

Make a collection of many types of containers that open and close in different ways. Possibilities: decorative metal tins with hinged lids; "fruitcake" metal boxes where the lid pulls off; old pressed powder compacts with hinged lids; plastic eggs that pull apart; small jewelry boxes; small change purses that open in different ways; match boxes with little drawers that slide out; a small jar with a screw-on lid; a plastic film canister; lunch boxes, a cloth bag with a draw-string; a small jewelry box with a latch on the lid; a margarine tub and lid. For extra fun, you might put little surprises inside the containers, such as pictures cut from magazines, or scented cotton balls. Put all these things in a larger, decorated box. Bring this out at special times for one or two children to play with. Children will enjoy opening and closing them and putting containers inside of other containers (Cognitive)

PEOPLE CLOTHESPINS

Materials:

Old-fashioned, non-spring wooden clothespins
Permanent ink marking pens
Coffee can with plastic lid

Use the permanent marking pens to draw faces, hair and clothing on the clothespins (adult job). Cut a hole ½ inch in diameter in the middle of the plastic lid of the coffee can. File off any sharp edges on the can. Store the clothespins in the can with the lid on. The child will enjoy prying off the plastic lid and dumping the clothespins out. Then the child can make the clothespin people straddle the edge of the can, lining them all up. When the child is through playing, he can put the lid back on the can and then have the fun of sticking all the clothespins through the hole to put them away.

STRINGING THINGS ON PLASTIC TUBING

Materials:

A variety of interesting things to string, such as large purchased wooden beads; tape spools; thread spools; hair curlers; round cereal; pasta.
Thin plastic tubing (such as aquarium tubing) available at hardware or pet stores.

Let children string beads and other things onto this tubing instead of the laces that come with the beads. They will be less frustrated, and achieve the same fine motor practice.

DIFFERENT DIAMETERS OF TUBING

Materials:

Plastic tubing of at least three different diameters (available in the plumbing department of hardware stores)—about 3 feet of each. Purchase sizes that will fit inside each other.

Cut the tubing into smaller pieces (or have the person at the hardware store do it for you), leaving the smallest diameter tubing the longest. Let children experiment with the different sizes, push-

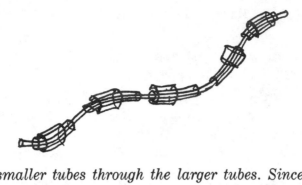

ing the smaller tubes through the larger tubes. Since the tubes are transparent, they will be able to see the smaller tubes inside the larger ones. (Congitive)

MODIFY DRESS-UP CLOTHES

Materials:

Sewing materials

Toddlers are very good at taking off clothes, but not as skilled at putting them on. Go through your collection of dress up clothes and remove the regular fasteners. Enlarge the button holes and stitch around the edges. Replace the regular buttons with large, colorful buttons. These will be more enticing for the child to use. Replace small zippers with large, plastic zippers. Difficult fasteners such as hooks and eyes could be replaced with velcro so the child can be independent. (Self.)

HAMMER GOLF TEES

Materials:

Golf tees
Solid block of styrofoam
Small wooden mallet from pounding toy

Let the child pound the golf tees into the styrofoam using a small wooden mallet that comes with a pounding bench toddler toy. Great fun! (Supervise so that the golf tees do not end up in ears or nostrils.)

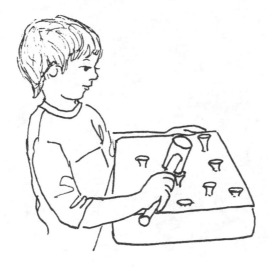

The Endless Pleasure of Playdough

Toddlers never seem to tire of playing with playdough, especially if you add plenty of variety. Make it up in different colors. Give children different objects to use with the dough. While they are enjoying this material, remember that they are benefiting by using their hand muscles and enjoying the cause and effect of their hand actions. See the "Cognitive" chapter for a recipe for homemade playdough, as well as several activities using playdough.

CUTTING PLAYDOUGH

Materials:

> *Playdough*
> *Blunt scissors*

To make scissors work correctly, a child must be able to open and close the hand and apply pressure. It's a very challenging skill, often not learned until the child is three. Children not yet able to use scissors successfully with paper will greatly enjoy cutting playdough. Show children how to roll long snakes of playdough. Then give them round-end scissors and let them snip pieces off the end, making many little pieces. You will be amazed at how long this activity will hold their attention. In the process,

they are practicing the hand muscle movements needed for success-ful cutting later.

BUILDING—COMBINING SHAPES TO MAKE THINGS

Creativity is combining things to make something new and using things in unusual ways. In that sense, toddlers are the most creative people on earth! We know that toddlers and two-year-olds love to combine things that fit together . . . and take them apart again. They make the discovery that the raised bumps on fit-together toys fit into the recessed holes in other pieces. They like to stack up blocks and knock them down again, or line up blocks or other objects in long rows.

At this stage of the game it is not really a creative process with the aim of making something, but rather, exploring the mechanical process of making things fit and seeing relationships. You can almost see the surprise on a child's face when he fits together two waffle shape blocks and discovers that they make a whole new shape. Then watch their pride when they make a whole long line of these.

Of course, this type of activity also gives children practice in developing their fine motor skills. And when they see relationships of spaces, shapes and sizes, they are gaining cognitive awareness. "Around the house" materials include such things as boxes of all types, small cans, plastic food storage boxes and bowls, cardboard cylinders and tubes, egg cartons, couch cushions, thread spools, even books. Very possibly a toddler in a home environment will discover these potential building materials before the adult does! When a child stacks up random combinations of objects she learns a bit about balance and gravity—"elementary physics."

As children gain experience with this type of material, it gradually changes from a random activity to an intentional activity. Rather than things happening by chance, the child will set out to do something particular with the material—to recreate a shape or pattern he happened upon before, or to imitate what he sees another child do. Then it becomes "creative." Children begin to learn that they combine shapes to make a whole new shape and they might even use their new shape in their play; for example, they decide their string of blocks is a "road."

To support this kind of creative play, try to provide children with a variety of interesting materials to combine. Avoid "giving assignments" or telling the child what to make. Instead, just let the child explore the materials and make discoveries on her own.

Manipulatives

In early childhood equipment supply catalogs, you will find a wide variety of manufactured toys that fit together, that give the child different kinds of fine motor practice. Make sure that the individual pieces of toys you make available to toddlers are large enough so that children cannot choke on them. These toys include large plastic fit-together brick sets, nesting and stacking cups, table blocks, counting cubes, star builders, and bristle blocks. Many such toys come in several sizes. Choose the larger versions. Avoid toys that have holes that are too small or fit together in ways that are more complex such as tinker toys, flexible straw builders or wooden log builders. These might frustrate rather than challenge children.

Blocks

Blocks also appeal to toddlers and two year olds. One of the first invented games of a toddler is to knock down blocks that an adult stacks up. Later, the child learns the fun of stacking up the blocks herself. Lining up the blocks end to end, or side by side also becomes interesting, and the child will enjoy pushing a toy truck along her "road." Small dolls or plastic animals might be placed on the blocks or inside enclosed spaces.

A variety of blocks can be purchased in early childhood equipment supply catalogs. Large plastic waffle shaped blocks have great appeal to toddlers. There are also large plastic fit-together blocks, vinyl-covered foam rubber blocks, smaller blocks made out of dense foam, and large cardboard blocks. Twos can also enjoy wooden unit blocks, but these may require closer supervision because they sometimes like to throw blocks.

An adult can support block play simply by sitting near-by and looking interested. Or, try "parallel playing" with the child. Sit on the floor near the child and play with the blocks. Mostly, take your lead from the child. Do what the child is doing with her blocks. The child might enjoy taking turns with you adding blocks to a stack or line. Before long, a two-year-old will discover how to make a wide range of interesting arrangements of materials and might even start labelling them as beds or roads or swimming pools. Then get ready to enjoy the pretend play that can result.

BLOCKS MADE OF DIAPER BOXES

Materials:

Disposable diaper boxes   *Masking tape*
Newspaper   *Decorative self-stick paper*

Let children help you make these blocks and then have the fun of playing with them. Simply wad up the newspaper, stuff it into the empty boxes, tape the boxes shut and cover the boxes with the self-stick paper (optional). Children feel powerful when they pick up and stack something that is large.

Activities related to building in *Things to Do with Toddlers and Twos:* pp. 92–95.

Activities related to fine motor development in *Things to Do with Toddlers and Twos:* pp. 89–92; 97; 104–115.

CHAPTER 10

Me, Myself, and I!

A dedicated teacher who works with toddlers said to me, "I've been reading a lot about the struggle of adults to rediscover the child inside of them . . . 'protect the inner child,' and so on. What I've come to realize is that these little children—these one and two year olds—*are* their own inner child. This stage is what it is all about."

This chapter is about a young child's personality development and helping a child develop a "positive self-image," a sense of who she or he is as an individual and as a valued member of a group. Practically everything in this book could conceivably be put into this chapter. It is almost impossible to separate this topic from social development and guidance. A child's expressions in dramatic play, creative activities, and language certainly are a reflection of how they see themselves. Even routine times of the day—diapering, dressing, napping, are times when a child interacts with important adults and develops feelings about his or her capabilities. There *is* no more important aspect of your teaching than nurturing children's emotional development—their sense of themselves. It is really woven into everything else that you do.

YOUR INTERACTIONS WITH CHILDREN

Children's self-image develops as a result of the way others respond to them. Interact with children so that they feel worthy and respected. After you read the pointers below, add to them. They are only starters.

- Greet the child warmly in the morning. Greet the parent warmly too—the parent is very much a part of the child's sense of identity.
- Use the child's name whenever you address him or her.
- Make eye contact with the child when you talk to her. It helps to get down on the child's level. Smile.
- Be conscious of your tone of voice when you talk to children. Be friendly and sincere without being "sugary." Be careful not to convey hostility in your tone.
- Make an effort to talk to the child one-on-one, many times during the day. Don't just address all your comments to the whole group. Take advantage of routine care times such as putting on coats, toileting, and handwashing for one-on-one conversations with children, and whenever else you can fit it in.
- Listen to the child's attempt to talk to you. See if you can extend his words into a conversation where you take turns talking.
- Touch the child often—a hand on the shoulder, a pat on the head, holding hands, a readily available lap. Physical contact is important to young children.
- Hug the child *when the child wants a hug*, not when *you* want a hug. If she looks forlorn or in need of comfort, ask "Would you like a hug?"
- Tell the child what you are going to do before you do it, and what comes next. Instead of swooping in from behind and picking up the child to go and get her diaper changed, approach from the front and say, "Amanda, it is time to change your diaper now, so I am going to pick you up and carry you over here."
- When you set limits and correct children do so in a firm, but friendly manner. "The table is not for standing on. Let's go over here to the climber." "Pulling hair hurts people, Mark. If you want to touch Sandy's hair touch it gently like this. See?" (See Guidance chapter.)

- Be responsive. When a child cries out for you, do what you can to help. Even if you are busy doing something else, like changing a diaper, respond verbally. "Yes Nadine, I hear you. I will come over and help you as soon as I am finished changing Lionel's diaper." "Be there" for the child when he needs assistance or is frightened.
- Interpret for the child. Help the child know she has communicated. "You want me to read this book to you? Sure . . . let's sit down over here."

All these things and more make children feel like "they count." They are important. You care about them.

PRETEND YOU ARE BEING OBSERVED

When you spend long hours with children it is easy to slip into habits of interactions with children that may not be as positive as they could or should be. One good way to stay on your toes is to pretend you are being observed by your director, a program supervisor, a parent, a child psychologist, a favorite college teacher, anyone else you respect. In fact, it may be good to ask one of these people to actually come and observe you for a period of time and give you feedback, just so you can see what it is really like. Or, try tape recording yourself. You are more likely to lower your tone of voice, speak more slowly, get down on the child's level and address children individually in appropriate ways. Try it—it's fun!

PLAY WITH CHILDREN

Dr. Stanley Greenspan in his book, *The Essential Partnership: How Parents and Children Can Meet the Emotional Challenges of Infancy and Childhood*, and in a video tape, *Floortime*, produced by Scholastic Inc., describes a process dubbed "Floortime." Not necessarily performed on the floor, it is a process by which an adult can connect with a child on an emotional level and become a partner in play. Children express themselves, especially their emotional selves, through their play. Feelings for which the child may not have the words are acted out when they crash cars, put babies to bed in the doll corner, or giggle and dump sand. Playing *with* a child gives you a real opportunity to peek through the window of play and see what is going on with the child. There are some specific techniques to keep in mind:

- It has to be "real" play that is *chosen by the child*. It's best if the child has a variety of play things to choose from. Then you can go over and sit next to him and gradually join in.
- It is best if this play is one-on-one and is sustained over a period of time. In a group care situation, this is easiest to accomplish during your "free-play time." Another child might spontaneously join you and that is okay, because there is great value in children learning to play together and you can be a good model of play skills.
- Make eye contact. Communicate as much through facial expressions and gestures as words.
- Join in to what the child is doing already. In other words, let the child set the agenda. If she is playing with a steering wheel and making motor noises, ask if you can go for a ride with her. If a child is pretending to cook, tell him you are hungry and would he fix you something to eat. If a child is building with blocks, you might start by building next to the child, trying to copy what the child has built.
- Follow the child's lead. It can start out as a simple, spontaneous "follow the leader" game. This works especially well with very young toddlers. A toddler in her play hits a hollow box with her hand three times to see what kind of noise it makes. You copy her action and also hit the box three times. Make eye contact and smile. The child will likely repeat the action and you have a game going. Or the child may go on to another action, such as hitting a different object, and you can again imitate the action. What the child subconsciously thinks is, "Hey . . . this person thinks my ideas are fun. I can make her do things. I have power. I am an interesting person."
- Let the child direct the action and tell you what to do. As you join her in the dramatic play corner, ask, "What should I wear?" Allow the child to dress you up. Ask about your role. "Am I the neighbor lady next door?" Be sure to let the child take on the dominant role and you can be a "supporting player."
- Do not be judgmental. If a child, for instance is spanking a

doll, do not say, "It's not nice to hit your baby. Be a nice mother." Instead, talk about what is happening. "This mommy seems to be mad at this baby. Why is the mommy mad?"

- Be an "announcer." Describe the child's play. "Here comes the car around the bend. It looks like it's going to crash into the building . . . oh no!"
- Ask questions. Expand on the child's ideas—with his concurrence. "Do we have everything we need to make this picnic? Do we need to pretend to go to the store?" "Where are we going on this bus?"

When you take time to play with children in this way, you will be amazed at the fun you have, personally. This is an extremely useful way to build a relationship with children. You are "validating" the child—letting the child know that he is interesting and fun to be with. In the process the child's vocabulary and play skills will grow and he will be better able to express emotions.

AUTONOMY

"I wanna do it *my byself!*" is one of the phrases of toddlerhood that stayed in the lore of my family. Whether it was pushing the button of an elevator, choosing what to wear in the morning or climbing the old apple tree in the back yard as a two-year-old, riding a two-wheeler or making brownies as a school-aged child, or driving a car as a teen-ager . . . this phrase indicated the determination of the child to prove she could do the task without adult assistance. Even if the task was a struggle for the child, the result was a sense of accomplishment that boosted the self-image and pride . . . when this parent had the patience to allow it.

The young toddler is asserting herself as an individual. She is sensing that she is independent from her parents and is testing how much she can really use her own will in situations. This accounts for the negativism that sometimes appears in children at this stage. When the child resists, she is proving she is separate from the parent to whom she has been bonded for so long and has her own will and can determine what she will and won't do.

Children are often more cooperative with child care providers than they are with their parents. They are not trying to prove they are separate from the child care provider. They already know that. Also, it's more fun to do what all the other children are doing. Toddlers' natural tendency toward parallel play helps.

However, toddlers and twos will also assert their independence with child care providers. A child may resist coming inside or putting a toy away when it is time to clean up for lunch. It is best to empathize with the child, acknowledging his feelings, but still expediting the matter. "I know, you wish we could stay out here longer, but Mary has lunch ready and it smells good, too." If the child does not cooperate after a tolerable interval, gently "assist" him, still acknowledging his feelings and stating your needs as well. Decide when it is okay to let the child "win." When there is a struggle, ask yourself if it is really important that you get your way.

The most important thing you can do to encourage children's development of autonomy—their sense of independence—is to give them many legitimate choices during the day. Don't control them all the time and tell them what to do every minute of the day. This is one reason for a good, long, enriched "free-play" or "free-choice" time when children can choose their own activities and who they will play with or near.

Offer children some options and go with their choices. "Shall we eat snack indoors or out on the playground today?" "Shall I put this picture over here by the window, or over there by the door?" "Which of these books should we read first?" "Would you rather have crayons or playdough out this morning?" This gives children a feeling of control.

BUILDING A FEELING OF INDEPENDENCE AND COMPETENCE

Take a look at your environment and see if there are some ways you can modify things to let children be more independent. Also, allow enough time for children to do things without your assistance. If you have trouble justifying the extra minutes this requires, remember that these are learning moments. They are just as important as planned curriculum portions of your day. Some possibilities:

- Make a step or two up to your sink so children can reach the faucet and the soap and wash their own hands.

- Place coat hooks within reach of children so they can pull off their own jackets when it is time to go outside and hang them up again.
- If necessary, place a step, or build one in, at your toilet so children don't have to be lifted onto the seat.
- Build a ramp up to your changing table so children can crawl up themselves. Let the child get his own diaper from an open bin within his reach.
- Have children scrape their own dishes after lunch, put their plates on a stack, and put silverware in a container of soapy water. They can also put their own napkin in the waste basket.
- Place toys on open shelves within children's reach so they don't have to ask you for everything or wait until you decide to make something available.
- Store toys in the same place every day, with picture labels so children know where to find things and put them away again.
- If a task is too difficult for the child to do independently, you do the first part and let the child do the last part. You start the zipper and let the child pull it the rest of the way up; you make the bow loops and let the child pull the bow tight on shoelaces.

THE DEVELOPMENT OF PRIDE

Some people think of pride as a negative personality trait. They associate it with vanity and self-centeredness. However, it is important that young children have a "baseline" of pride—of feeling good about who they are . . . valued members of the social group. Parents and family members have the first, critical role here. It is the feeling that is communicated: "You are the most wonderful miracle on earth!" The unconditional love and admiration parents and grandparents give children is invaluable in developing the child's self-image.

Even though you are not the emotionally involved parent, as a trusted and cherished caregiver, you are very important to the child's development of pride. The longer you are with the child, the more this is true, and contrary to some popular notions, in my experience I find that caregivers *do* get emotionally involved with the children in their care. (In fact, many teachers of toddlers have told me that is what keeps them working with this age.)

When a child accomplishes a new skill and the admiring adult says, "Look at you! You did it by yourself!" the child will beam with the pride of accomplishment. Try to catch your toddlers at moments of accomplishment and reinforce their pride in the task. Let them bask in your admiration. If parents are depressed or terribly stressed they may forget to "shine" on the child in this way. The help and support of caring professionals can help "teach" them how to respond.

BECOME A BROADCASTER

Magda Gerber suggests that rather than giving out endless bland praise, adults should become "broadcasters," or "announcers" of children's activities and accomplishments. "Jessica has buttoned her coat!" "Marvin has climbed to the top of the climber." "Max colored his crayons all over the piece of paper and made lots and lots of lines." She also recommends praising children for doing things that are very hard for toddlers to do. For waiting patiently. For giving up a toy so someone else can have a turn. For asking for something rather than grabbing it. For touching a friend gently. Different children will deserve praise for different actions that are personally difficult for them.

PRAISE GOOD THINKING

Grace Mitchell advocates praising children for having good ideas, rather than commenting on a child's looks or what the child is wearing. "You used the box top to make a roof for your blocks. What a good idea!" "I like the way you think!"

HELP STOP THE EARLY DEVELOPMENT OF PREJUDICE

Two year olds are gathering basic information about the gender, race, ethnicity and varying physical abilities of themselves and others. This is all part of the development of their sense of identity. In her book, *Anti-Bias Curriculum, Tools for Empowering Young Children*, Louise Derman-Sparks, along with the A.B.C. Task

Force, examines these identity issues for two year olds in a special chapter.

Young children are sometimes uncomfortable around people who are different from them, and generally prefer playmates who are most like them. This may be caused by fear of the unfamiliar. You, a trusted adult, have much influence in what a child will find interesting and acceptable in other people.

Sex Roles

By the time they are two, most children know if they are boys or girls, but they may be confused as to what *makes* them boys or girls. They may often think that length of hair, or the type of clothing they wear, influences their gender. You will see much curiosity and looking at diapering and toileting times, and children will occasionally ask questions or comment on genitals.

It is important not to laugh at their questions or comments or reprimand children for making them. Instead, simply give them factual information. "Martin has a penis. He is a boy." "Girls don't have penises. They have a vagina." Having "anatomically correct" dolls in your program is one way to give children opportunities to ask questions and learn about gender differences in appropriate ways.

It is at this age that children also start absorbing some cultural stereotypes of what males and females can and cannot do in our society. Make an effort to expose children to a wide range of role models. Through fathers and male staff members in your program, for instance, they should see that men can be loving and nurturing to young children. Also help them be aware of men and women in occupations of all types.

PICTURES

Find pictures to put up in your room of people in "non-traditional" work—women in construction jobs or driving large vehicles; men cooking, working with children, cleaning house.

DRAMATIC PLAY OPPORTUNITIES

In your dramatic play area, provide props appropriate for all types of roles, and encourage both boys and girls to play with

*them. As well as the traditional "house play" props like dishes,
dolls and cleaning things, provide such things as briefcases, an
old typewriter or computer keyboard, hard hat, lunch box, tools,
and other artifacts of the work world.*

Racial Awareness

A fact to remember is that young children *do* notice physical
attributes of people. To say that little children do not notice race
is simply a fallacy. They may not yet have the *words* to describe
what they notice, but their interest and curiosity is there.

ADMIRING MIRROR

Materials:

A tall mirror that stands on the floor

*Gather a small group of children in front of the mirror. Look at
each child in the mirror together and talk about that child's physical
characteristics in descriptive admiring terms. "Jennifer's skin is
a light color and her hair is very silky and soft. The color of her
hair is called blond. And her eyes are light blue." "Now Martin
here has very shiny straight black hair and his eyes are very
dark brown. Martin's skin is a beautiful light brown." "Samantha
has beautiful dark brown skin. Her eyes are big and brown and
her hair is black and curly with pretty braids in it." "Let's all
put our arms right here and look at all the pretty colors of skin
we have."*

DIFFERENT KINDS OF HAIR

Materials:

Instant camera (optional)
Dolls with hair (optional)   *Magazines (optional)*

*See how many different kinds of hair you can find in the children,
staff and parents in your program. Ask people if they will allow
the children to look at and touch their hair. Teach children to
ask others if they can touch their hair. Can you find grey, curly
hair; black, straight hair; brown, short hair; braided hair; twisted
hair; pony tails? Try to find some men with long hair and women*

with very short hair, so that children lessen their associations of gender with length of hair. Let the people talk about how they take care of their hair and what they use to hold it in place. If possible, take a picture of the hair of all these people. Children could later wash the hair of dolls and comb it. They could also page through magazines to see all the different kinds of hair they can find in pictures and talk about it. The point of the activity is to develop the idea that there are many kinds of hair people have on their heads, and all of it is beautiful.

Pictures and Dolls

Children should see themselves reflected in the materials around them. Make sure you have pictures, books and dolls that represent the races of all the children in your group. If your group is all one race, there should be other races represented as well.

Be on the look-out for magazine pictures of people of different races. More magazines are becoming socially conscious in this way. *Pre-K Today* magazine, published by Scholastic Inc. is one excellent source of pictures of children.

Major early childhood equipment catalogs now have a wide variety of dolls that respectfully and charmingly represent different races. You can also ask parents and volunteers to help make some cloth dolls using different "skin" colors of fabric.

WASHING OFF DIRT

Materials:

Dolls of different skin colors	Soap
Mud	Wash cloth
Water table, sink or dish tubs	Adult with dark skin color

Young children sometimes think dark skin is dark because it is dirty. This activity is designed to show them that there is a difference between dirt and skin color. In the process, stress that all skin colors are pretty.

Put mud on the dolls, if they are not already dirty. Also ask the adult with dark skin to put some mud on his or her hands. Provide warm water and soap so children can wash the dolls. While they are enjoying the process, notice how the dirt comes off, but skin color does not come off. Have them notice especially the person with dark skin color. Say "The mud and dirt came off, but Martha's skin is still a pretty brown because that is the color of her skin. That doesn't wash off." Notice whatever variety there is in the color of the skin of the children as well.

Disabilities

Disabilities are sometimes frightening to very young children. They may be afraid that if they play with a disabled child they, too, will develop a disability. Answer their questions as matter-of-factly and factually as possible. "The muscles in Brian's leg are weak. His brace helps him stand up."

If you have a child with a disability in your program, include the child in all the normal activities of the group, offering assistance only when it is needed. Stress what the child *can* do. When you see other children staring or acting uncomfortable, try to guess what is causing their behavior and explain as simply and as factually as possible, without making the child with the disability feel conspicuous.

It is important to include the topic of people with disabilities with any group of children over time, because it is part of the world they live in. If children are exposed early to the idea that people have different abilities, they are more likely to accept people with disabilities without prejudice or fear when they encounter them in real life situations.

There are now dolls with disabilities on the market—dolls with hearing aids, leg braces, even wheel-chairs. For a catalog, write to Hal's Pals, P.O. Box 3490, Winter Park, CO 80482. Phone: 303–726–8388. If these dolls stretch your budget, consider trying to make some. Children with disabilities themselves may feel self-conscious having other children examine their mechanical aids. A doll allows other children to express their curiosity without causing embarrassment to the disabled child. Dolls are also a way to introduce the concept of people with disabilities to groups where there is not a child with a disability present.

Children's Books About Disabilities

There are more and more excellent books about people with disabilities on the market. If you find some that are aimed at slightly older children, "tell" the book to your children rather than reading it, adjusting the vocabulary and concepts so they can understand, while letting them look at the picture.

RESOURCES

Books:

Derman-Sparks, Louise, *Anti-Bias Curriculum*, NAEYC. 1988.
There is an excellent reference section of recommended children's books, and curriculum materials, as well as a whole chapter on working with two-year-olds.

Gerber, Magda. *A Manual for Parents and Professionals*. Publ. by Resources for Infant Educarers, 1550 Murray Circle, L.A., CA 90026. 6th printing, 1987.
This is a general manual that covers all aspects of caring for infants and toddlers. It has undercurrents of respect for children and their individual differences.

Greenspan, Stanley and Nancy Thorndike Greenspan, *The Essential Partnership—How Parents and Children Can Meet the Emotional Challenges of Infancy and Childhood*. Viking Penguin, Inc. 1989.
Descriptions of children's stages of emotional development and how the adult can support.

Video tape:

Greenspan, Stanley, *Floortime*, Scholastic Inc. 1990.
Taped in a child care setting as well as in homes, this video demonstrates how and why to connect with children through play.

CHAPTER 11

It's Great to Have Friends!

- Todd, new to the child care center, is crying loudly because Mommy left. Four other children stop what they are doing, come over and stare at him and look sad. Molly gives him her blanket.

- A visitor comes into the room and sits down on a chair to observe for a few minutes. Peter comes over and gives her a block. He continues to bring her other toys. Later, when she leaves the room, there are waves and a chorus of "Bye-bye!"

- Mindy takes her shovel and hits the sand three times, saying, "Bang, bang, bang." Paul, digging near-by, stops digging and hits his shovel on the ground three times and says, "Bang, bang, bang!" They look at each other and laugh.

These are all examples of early social behaviors of toddlers. Older infants see their peers as interesting "objects," great for their experiments in cause and effect. An inquisitive 11 month old is as likely to grab a handful of someone's cheek, or put a finger in an eye, as she is to grab the glasses off her grandfather. Gradually, as children acquire language and experience with other children, their world expands. Their interactions start out with non-verbal games and routines. They will imitate each other's actions. They will enjoy the social feeling of belonging. They begin to develop empathy—the ability to feel for someone else—and they learn how their actions affect the feelings and actions of others. With the gentle guidance of caring adults they can begin to learn the social give and take of sharing and taking turns and expressing their needs appropriately. Soon they are enjoying having fun with their friends.

ENJOYING THE GROUP EXPERIENCE

Learning to enjoy being one among others is one of the challenges for toddlers and two-year-olds in group care. The hard parts are learning to wait and take turns from time to time, and share the attention of the adults. But the good part is learning the pleasure of having friends and a feeling of belonging. Children develop positive social patterns most easily if their group is fairly small— 8 to 12 children, and the group members, adults as well as children, are consistent. This section will describe a few ways to build a sense of pleasant group belonging.

The Sweet Sound of Your Own Name

Even as adults, we start to feel like we "belong" or are legitimate members of a group when we know the names of others present, and they know our names. A key line in the theme song to the popular television show, "Cheers," mentions, "a place where everybody knows your name." Try to use children's names whenever you talk to them. Here are a few other fun ways to help children learn and use the names of the other children in the group.

Enthusiastic Greeting Using Names

As each child arrives, say, "Look, everybody, here is our friend, *Kimmy!* Good morning, Kimmy." Encourage the other children to say hi or good morning to the arriving child as well. This develops feelings of friendship and belonging. Always greet the adult bringing the child as well as the child. You are creating a good liaison between home and classroom by demonstrating friendly feelings with the child's family.

If you arrive after some of the children, go around to each and greet him or her personally. Touch the child on the shoulder or head as you say hello and say their name. Make that initial personal contact part of your every day arrival ritual. This helps children feel "counted" or acknowledged, and they will be less likely to engage in behaviors just to get your attention.

Likewise, when a child leaves, encourage other children to say good-by using his name. "Jason is leaving now. Let's say good-bye. Bye-bye, Jason. See you tomorrow." Accompany this with a wave. The children will imitate you, and Jason and his parent will probably wave back and leave with a warm feeling of being valued.

GROUP MEMBER DOOR POSTER

Materials:

2 pieces of poster board	*Scissors*
Photograph of each child,	*Tape*
staff, classroom pet	*Yarn*

On one of the poster boards, cut flaps or "doors," the size of the photographs, for each child in your group. Include your own picture, and that of other staff members, your pet puppet, and classroom pets. Punch a little hole and put a small loop of yarn through it in each door to make it easier to open. Place this piece of posterboard over the second, uncut piece. Trace the outlines of the doors onto the bottom posterboard to mark their location. Then glue the photographs of the children on the marked spaces of the bottom board. Tape the two pieces together. Decorate the top board any way you wish.

Take the children over to the door board. Say, "I wonder whose picture is behind this door." Invite a child to open the flap. "Who is that?" "Yes, it's Kimmy!" "See, here is our friend Kimmy, and here is her picture." "Which door shall we try next?"

This activity helps children learn each other's names. You will also be amazed at how quickly they memorize the location of the pictures. Hang this board somewhere in your classroom, where children can reach it and play with it on their own.

CLASS PHOTO ALBUM

Take pictures of the children in your group doing all sorts of everyday and special activities. Keep them in a photo album with magnetic plastic pages, and place the album where children can look at it—with your other books perhaps. It will be their favorite book to "read." You can talk about the pictures with them, using the names of the children, and giving valuable language practice as you and they describe the pictures. "Who is this?" "Why is Martin wearing a heavy jacket?" "Look—here is Maria with yellow paint all over her hands. Maria is having fun painting in this picture." (Cognitive, Language, Self)

"WHO'S HERE TODAY" PICTURE TO PERSON GAME
Materials:

A photograph of each child
Clear self-adhesive plastic or laminate
Bag
Poster board with "pockets" for each picture, which allows most of the picture to show. Label the board, "Who's Here Today."

Shoebox with a lid with a slot cut in it. Label the box, "Not here today."

Laminate, or cover pictures with clear self-adhesive plastic for durability. Put all the pictures in a bag. Gather all the children in a group. One at a time, let the children come to you and pull one picture out of the bag. Ask, "Who is this?" If necessary, prompt the child with the correct name. "That is Alberto, isn't it?" "Can you find Alberto? Is he here today? Bring the picture over to Alberto." Then let Alberto put his own picture in one of the pockets in your "Who's Here Today" poster board. If the child in the photo is not present, let the child who pulled out the photo put this photo through the slot into the shoebox labelled "not here." (If the child comes in later, she can find her own photo in the box and place it in a pocket on the board.)

This activity not only gives children social contact with each other and helps them learn names, it is also a good cognitive activity. A photograph is a "symbol" of a person. A child is learning to associate a symbol with the thing it represents—the real person. And by looking at the photo, the child can form a mental image of the friend who is not there. (Self, Cognitive)

SONGS INVOLVING NAMES

Pick any familiar melody, such as "Twinkle, Twinkle, Little Star," and instead of singing the words, chant a child's name with the children. The child whose name is being chanted can get up and jump up and down.

In familiar songs, substitute children's names for characters in the song. "Lionel had a little lamb . . . ."

Sing "Theresa in the Dell." Instead of having the "farmer" pick animals, have Theresa pick another child. Then sing, "Theresa picked a Paul, Theresa picked a Paul, Hi-ho-the-derry-o, Theresa picked a Paul." Then have Paul pick someone, and continue this type of sequence until every child has been chosen and sung about. (Self)

PET PUPPET GREETINGS

Materials:

Hand puppet that will become a "class pet"

Have the puppet come out and greet each child personally each morning. Start with a formal introduction to each child. "Flopsy, I would like you to meet Debbie." Then the puppet can give Debbie a kiss.

FORGETFUL PUPPET

Materials:

Pet puppet

The puppet comes out and says he forgot the names of some of the children in the group and wants help remembering. So have each child stand up in turn, and tell the puppet his name. He repeats the name. You talk about other ways he can remember who is who. Describe each child. "Now remember, Flopsy, this is Jamie. You can remember Jamie because he has big brown eyes and black curly hair." The puppet ends up saying everybody's name correctly. (Language)

LEARNING TO SHARE AND TAKE TURNS

One of the many things parents want when they enroll their children in child care centers is for their children to learn to share and take turns. Often teachers wish children would hurry up and learn this too!

Why is this so difficult for children? Why is it that with a room full of toys, the toddler wants only what the child next to her has? Why is it so difficult to turn over the riding toy to someone else on the playground? Keep some of these developmental issues in mind as you try to understand the actions of toddlers:

- Toddlers and two-year-olds are ego-centric. They haven't learned to put themselves in someone else's shoes. All they know is they WANT that toy. So they take it.
- Toddlers are impulsive. They don't do a lot of advance planning but often simply want what they see right now—in the hands of another child.
- Often it seems not to be the coveted toy that they really want. They are experimenting with social dominance. "Can I control this other person?"

- Toddlers haven't learned about "reciprocity"—"You scratch my back, I'll scratch yours." And in reality, this often doesn't work. They hand a toy over, and nothing nice happens back. The other child takes the toy and won't give it back later. It takes a lot of experiences with other children, and some gentle coaching from adults to learn the give and take of social situations.
- Children have a very vague concept of time. To wait five minutes for a turn can seem like forever to a two-year-old.

What can teachers do to help children learn to share and take turns and generally be more considerate of each other?

- Be aware of your influence as a model. Do some sharing yourself, and talk about it so that children learn what it *is*. "I know you like oranges, so I brought some to share with you." "Natalie and I are sharing these crayons."
- Allow children to really "possess" an object first and give it up on their own terms. For instance, a child is playing with a toy truck and another child wants it. Say, "Joshua has that now. Joshua, will you please tell Angela when you are through playing with it so she can have a turn?" The possessor often gives up the toy in a surprisingly short time. But it is *his* decision, and he is in control. Also, allow enough time for a child to really enjoy the toy. One ride around the circle on the tricycle will not be satisfying, and it will be much harder to turn it over than if the child has had a longer time with the trike.
- Praise sharing behaviors in children. "You boys are doing a good job sharing the pegs."
- Point out how others feel when you share with them. "That made Natalie happy when you let her have a turn on the swing."
- Have enough toys to occupy other children while they are waiting. Don't expect eleven children to share three sand buckets.
- Resist the temptation just to take over and dictate. Don't get into the "Who had it first?" game. It will lead you nowhere. Ask yourself, "What can be taught here?" Teach negotiation skills. It helps if you have some interesting activity for the waiting child.
- Maybe the waiting child can find a toy to offer to trade for the coveted item.

• During your group time, have a nice, neutral discussion about sharing, with your pet puppet. The puppet could tell how he wanted to play with clay but his brother had all of it and he felt sad. Then the teacher and the children could suggest things the puppet could do.

Of course, none of these things work all of the time, and some of them will work better with two-year-olds than with less experienced and less verbal toddlers. Sharing and taking turns are skills that are learned over a long period of time.

Set Up Some "Easy" Sharing and Turn-Taking Situations

The following simple activities or "set-ups" allow children to experience success in sharing and taking turns. Be sure to comment positively so they become conscious of the pleasant aspects of cooperation.

SHARING PEGS

Materials:

Large rubber peg boards   *Large pegs in one bowl*

Give two children their own peg boards and put the bowl of pegs between them. There are plenty of pegs and they each have their own space. Then comment on their sharing.

SHARING CRAYONS

Materials:

Paper   *Crayons in one basket*

Give each child a piece of paper and put the basket of crayons between them. You are building success experiences involved with sharing. Children will enjoy the social interactions.

TAKING TURNS WITH MANIPULATIVES

Materials:

Manipulative toys such as large pop beads, pegs, fit-together toys

With your guidance, let two children take turns adding a peg to a single peg board. Or let two children take turns pulling a pop bead or fit-together toy off a long chain. Then have them alternate putting them back on. Have two children take turns putting manipulatives pieces into a box with a slot top.

LEARNING EMPATHY—TEACH CHILDREN TO BE CONSIDERATE OF OTHERS THROUGH YOUR OWN MODEL

As mentioned earlier, children naturally start out "egocentric"—thinking only of themselves. Children gradually learn to have empathy—to feel for others and put themselves in their shoes—by watching adults behave that way. The most powerful models for learning social behaviors are their parents and their trusted caregivers. You have great influence.

TEACH CHILDREN TO BE COMFORTERS

You have probably noticed that when a child falls down and hurts himself in your program, the other children stop and watch. It is not all "morbid curiosity" that rivets their attention. They are also watching you and how you comfort the hurt child. They see you go over and stroke the child and offer sympathetic words. You can take advantage of this unplanned learning opportunity by involving the other children as well. "Oh look. Sara is crying. She fell down and bumped her knee. It hurt her. What can we do to make Sara feel better?" As you comfort Sara, other children might come and put their arms around her or give her a kiss. (You will have to judge if Sara is ready for such affections.) Someone might even bring her his blanket. Children tend to comfort others the way they, themselves have been comforted. You can reinforce such behaviors by saying, "That made Sara feel good when you gave her your blanket."

Children also watch how you comfort children who are sad or having a difficult time separating from their parent. You can use the same technique and involve the other children in making the sad child feel better by offering sympathy and comfort.

TING BEHAVIORS

...g children empathy and kindness, it is important that you do not allow children to hurt each other. Toddlers *are* often aggressive and push, bite, hit, scratch, pull hair, and otherwise use force to get what they want. React immediately, without mixed messages, when a child is hurting another child. "No hurting, Jamie. It hurts Jennifer when you pull her hair." It's important to be as consistent as possible in stopping such behaviors. If you ignore a hurting behavior, such as hitting or pushing or scratching, the children think that it's okay to do that—or even that you *condone* it. While you comfort the victim, help the child who was doing the hurting think of other ways to get what he wanted. (See Guidance chapter.)

It goes without saying that you yourself must not engage in hurting behaviors. Remember, children learn social behaviors by watching adult models. If hitting or spanking is what children witness admired adults doing, that is what they themselves will do to get what they want or express their anger. Instead, teach other strategies.

INTERPRETING CHILDREN TO EACH OTHER

Children learn friendship skills through interaction. Describe the feelings of the other child. This will help children to learn the "cause and effect" of social behaviors more quickly.

"Johnny didn't like it when you hit him. That's why he doesn't want to sit next to you now."

"Julius is crying because he is mad. It made him mad when you took that away from him."

Sometimes children fail to notice the positive overtures and behaviors of other children. You can act as an "interpreter," helping children notice and "read" each other's behavior correctly.

"Jennifer said she wants that chair. She wants you to help her get it. Can you help her, Mark?"

"Beth smiled when you gave her the bunny. It made her happy. She wants to play with you now."

"Look, Abby. Cal wants to play with you. He wants to put a block next to yours."

"Susan wants to get in the rocking boat with you. She said, 'Wait.' That means she wants you to stop the boat so she can get in."

BE A MODEL FOR PROBLEM SOLVING

A normal day with toddlers presents many problems to solve. Let children in on the process. Model problem solving yourself. Occasionally stage a social problem with another adult. "Katie and I both want to read this book to Christopher. What can we do? What if I read the first half of the book and she reads the second half? Then we will both be happy."

Use the same process in helping children with their problems. "Hmmm. There seems to be a problem here. Looks like both of you want to play with that truck, but Annie had it first. What can we do? Martha, would you like to play with this other truck near Annie so you can both play together?"

You are guiding children in successful social problem solving experiences. Later they will be able to do this sometimes without your guidance.

Don't step in too early. When you notice children in a conflict situation, see if they can figure it out themselves first.

HAVING FUN WITH OTHERS

"Solitary Play" is the dominant play style of younger toddlers. Although they are aware of the other children in the room, they pay little attention to them and simply go off on their own, happily digging or exploring a toy by themselves. (It is perfectly normal and acceptable for children of all ages to revert to solitary play from time to time.)

"Parallel Play" emerges as children gain experience being in groups of others close to their own age. You sense that children enjoy being together. They move close to each other and enjoy doing the same types of things the other children are doing. They imitate their friends and get ideas from each other. One child starts pouring sand down the slide. Soon three children are pouring sand down the slide.

Equipment for More Than One

To emphasize the fun part of being with others, try to plan activities that are more fun to do with other children than alone. Look for toys and equipment that accommodate more than one child so that children can get used to having fun together.

- A small playhouse, a converted appliance box, even a blanket thrown over a card table, invite several children to play together.
- The "Buddy Bike" manufactured by Angeles Nursery Toys is a feet-on-the-ground riding toy that has a long seat that accommodates two riders.
- Horizontal tire swings accommodate three children as they swing.
- Community Playthings' "Wagon for Six" and Angeles Nursery Toys' "Bye Buggy" allow caregivers to take several children for a ride at one time.
- A wooden rocking boat only rocks if there are at least two children in it. It's a favorite toddler toy that teaches positive social interaction.
- Community Playthings' "Driving Bench" has three steering wheels, so the children can parallel play and each be the "driver" and make driving noises at the same time.
- A safe, stable indoor climber or slide structure invites several children at a time to engage in spontaneous play.
- A wagon invites cooperation as one child rides and the other child pulls.
- A parachute is only fun to play with if several children work together. Then it's wonderful fun for older twos!
- Create small, cozy spaces in your environment, just right for two or three children to get into.
- A large sandbox encourages parallel play.

Interactive Activities

INNERTUBE BOUNCER

Materials:

Large tractor tire innertube	*Electric tape or duct tape*

After the inner tube is inflated, bend the valve back and tape it to the innertube. The tape can go all the way around the tube. This prevents the valve from poking someone. Several children can straddle the innertube and pretend to ride a horse. It's more fun when several children ride at once because there are extra bounces and jiggles. "Giddyup!"

FOLLOW THE LEADER

Any kind of game where children imitate each other is good for building social relationships. It's fun to be the leader and decide what everybody else will do. It is also fun to imitate and show you are one of the group and can do what everybody else can do.

CIRCLE GAMES

Simple, traditional circle games like "Ring Around the Rosie," "Hokey Pokey" and "Here We Go Round the Mulberry Bush" give children fun experiences of being part of a group, doing what everybody else is doing. They are gaining pleasure in shared experiences.

GROUP SINGING AND FINGERPLAYS

Singing simple songs together—the old favorites such as "Old Mac Donald," or "Twinkle, Twinkle, Little Star," or doing some familiar finger plays in a teacher-led group can also give a child a sense of belonging and pleasure in doing things with others. Dancing together, playing rhythm instruments are other examples.

GUIDED DRAMATIC PLAY

The "Bear Hunt" is an example of a guided dramatic play. It is a favorite action game because children don't have to be able to recite all the words, but can do the hand actions imitating the teacher and enjoy the excitement at the end.

Other simple examples are pretending to drive to a local fast food restaurant together. You might be sitting on your climber outside or sitting in chairs children have lined up in the room.

The teacher might lead pretend actions while children imitate—
like turning on the car, making car noises, steering, honking
the horn, placing the order, paying and enjoying the hamburger.
Again, these activities are more fun to do with a group than all
by yourself.

ROLL THAT BIG BALL BACK AND FORTH

Materials:

Ball

Seat the children in a circle and roll a ball back and forth while
you sing:

> *"Roll that big ball back and forth,*
> *Roll that big ball back and forth,*
> *Roll that big ball back and forth,*
> *OH, roll that big ball all around."*

(Use any melody that fits.) This is a good activity for learning
to be part of a group activity and take turns. At first, some young
toddlers might have trouble "giving up" the ball when it comes
to them, but they soon find out that the game is more fun if he
then rolls it back into the circle again. Have another ball to put
into play in case this happens. When the child does finally roll
the ball back out, make sure it gets back to him quickly so he
learns that it is not lost forever.

BECOMING AWARE OF THE WIDER WORLD

Part of social development is learning how one fits "in society."
Who are the other people around you? What roles do they play?
How do people depend on each other and help each other out?

Many programs for toddlers have experienced the one outside
event that brings all activity to a stop—the arrival of the garbage
truck. Without a doubt, it can be the most exciting event of the
week! One program was lucky enough to have a trash collector
who caught on and played up the show. He always waited until
he was at the child care center to compact the load of trash. Children
would line up at the windows or at the fence and clap and cheer,
watching the huge truck lift and empty the dumpster and smash
up the garbage, all the while making the most wonderful noise.

The trash collector and his crew always waved at the children. Eventually they arrived wearing funny hats to the great amusement of children and adults alike. Even if your trash collector is not this dramatic or this social, you can share the children's interest and talk about the important work he is doing.

Rather than build an abstract "theme unit" around "community helpers," point out to your children people and their jobs when they happen in real life. Young children are especially interested in people who wear uniforms or who use special equipment. Point out and recognize the cook in your center, the mail carrier in your neighborhood, delivery people, the visiting nurse. Talk about what these people do. Invite these people to spend a few moments with the children. Perhaps provide a few props so children can play some of these roles in their dramatic play.

KEEPING AN ANTI-BIAS FOCUS

In talking about people in the community and their roles, be sure that children see both men and women doing all types of work. Try to expose children to people of different races as well as disabled people working in the community. (See *Anti-Bias Curriculum* in resources below.)

RESOURCES

Crary, Elizabeth: *Kids Can Cooperate—A Practical Guide to Teaching Problem Solving*. Parenting Press, Inc. 1984.
This resource for adults discusses strategies for helping children learn to solve problems and get along. Although much of the book is aimed at working with preschoolers and school-age children, there is a section on toddlers, and it is worthwhile reading.

Derman-Sparks, Louise. *Anti-Bias Curriculum*. NAEYC. 1988.
An essential resource for early childhood programs, this book gives teachers much guidance on social issues of all types. There is a whole section on working with toddlers.

Edwards, Carolyn Pope: *Social and Moral Development in Young Children*. Teachers' College Press, New York, 1986.
This book provides the reader with insights to children's thinking from a Piagetian point of view, and gives teachers strategies for exposing children to social concepts. It helps a teacher realize what concepts a child can and cannot understand.

CHAPTER 12

What Shall We Do Today?

This book offers many fun activities to do with young children. But you need a "framework," a plan for making it all happen. This chapter is about "pulling it all together." Creating a good program for toddlers and twos requires planning, flexibility, and an understanding of how children learn. There are many ways to "do it right." You must figure out what is appropriate for your situation.

Your "curriculum" is all the planned activities that comprise your learning program for children. Children also learn much from accumulation of daily interactions with adults and other children— the conversations during diapering time, the problem solving when there is a dispute, the descriptions of the food at lunchtime, the spontaneous "happenings." In other words, there is a "planned curriculum" and a "spontaneous curriculum." Each is just as important as the other. Try to maintain an awareness of the learning potential in everything that happens.

KNOW HOW YOUNG CHILDREN LEARN

As you plan, keep in mind these things about how toddlers and two-year-olds learn:

- Toddlers cannot comprehend concepts they cannot see, hear, taste, smell or touch. So give your possible topics and activities the "senses test." The more senses you can involve in presenting a concept, the greater the likelihood for learning.

- Toddlers don't learn from the printed page. Stay away from coloring book type pages, workbooks, duplicated worksheets, patterns to complete. If you are ever tempted to use a worksheet, ask yourself what concept it is presenting, and think of ways to present that concept using real objects the children can touch.

- Toddlers have "object hunger." They have a drive to gain "physical knowledge" of the world they live in by examining every object they come across. Give them many interesting objects to examine and manipulate.

- Remember the "novelty factor." Young children are interested in anything that is "new" to the environment.

- Children like repetition of the familiar. They especially love repeating songs, fingerplays and simple games they know well, as well as favorite art projects. It gives them a feeling of mastery, and learning is solidified.

- Children learn most from activities they choose themselves. When their own interest motivates them to find out about something, they are more likely to remember what they learned. So schedule plenty of "free choice" time with interesting things for children to choose from.

DEVELOP A FOCUS FOR YOUR PLANNING

Start with the Interests of Individual Children

Plan your curriculum, taking off from the interests and abilities of children in your own group. Start by observing what they really do and are attracted to. Then think of more ways you can expose the child to that particular concept. When you plan activities with individual children in mind you are very likely to match the needs and interests of other children as well.

Is Manuel drawn to the cars and trucks in your block corner? Obtain or borrow more toy vehicles for him to play with and talk about them. Invite him to bring them to the sandbox. Collect pictures of all kinds of vehicles to show him and put them in a homemade book. Find library books about vehicles. Collect boxes, pieces of stiff cardboard, etc. that can be added to the block area to make tunnels and ramps. Take a few children for a short walk in your parking lot or neighborhood and look at all the different kinds of cars. When you are outside, notice the different kinds of vehicles in passing traffic.

Does Susan pretend to cook and feed babies? Pretend to be a baby and ask her to feed you. Bring in empty boxes and cans for her to pretend with. Find different pots and things to pretend to stir with. Visit the kitchen in your center, if your licensing regulations allow it, and allow her to watch cooking in action for brief amounts of time. Ask the cook to describe what she or he is doing. If you are a family child care provider, invite Susan to help you make lunch. Do some real cooking projects with a small group of children. Go on a trip to the grocery store with a small group.

To Theme or Not to Theme?

Many people like to develop their curriculum around "themes" or "units." A variety of activities are planned to give children experiences with the topic. For instance, if "farm animals" is the theme, in a given time children might take a trip to a farm or farm animals might be brought to visit the children at the center. Plastic farm animals might be added to the block area, and books and pictures of farm animals to the book corner. There are pros and cons to this type of planning.

Pros:
- This approach can broaden children's understanding of certain concepts. They are likely to know more about farm animals than when they started.
- Many senses are involved as concepts are presented through a number of different activities and play materials.
- It keeps *adults* interested. Sometimes the day to day caregiving of very young children can become boring to adults. By preparing a set of experiences around a topic and watching children respond, the adults learn more about the children and have more fun.

- Parents may feel more confident that children are actually "learning something."

Cons:

- The theme may become "an end in itself." Instead of focusing on children's interests, teachers may focus on getting all the activities done to present the theme they thought of.
- The theme may not be appropriate for the age level. This is sometimes true in programs that dictate a theme that the whole center must focus on for, say, a week at a time. A good theme for five year olds may not be just right for toddlers, and vice-versa.
- Adults are sometimes tempted to offer "final product" art projects to coordinate with the theme, for example, asking that children draw a picture of a farm animal, or color in a farm animal outline. This type of art project is meaningless for this age group.
- Caregivers may focus on the "externals," room decorations, for instance, instead of on what is really happening with the children.
- Caregivers may be less likely to lay aside their pre-planned activities for spontaneous happenings and interests of the children.
- Programs may impose an arbitrary time limit to themes. Children's interest in a topic might involve them for longer or shorter periods of time. When a theme is "finished" in the adult's time schedule, often things are put away forever as they move on to a different topic. This does not reflect how children learn or encourage their in-depth interest.
- Caregivers may think that everything they offer the children must coordinate with the theme. There are many basic activities—scribbling, playing with balls, dancing to music, poking playdough, playing with water—that are good to have available to children any time. These basics must not be neglected.

Do's and Don'ts for Developing Appropriate Curriculum Themes

Do:

- Generate possible topics. Themes should be expansions of the child's real world. Remember to give the topic the "senses test." Can children perceive it with their senses? Some possible theme topics: Bedtime; Pets; Clothing; The Grocery Store; Getting Things Clean; Vehicles.

- Develop themes that grow out of interest demonstrated spontaneously by children. This is ideal. Or, perhaps you can "create" some "spontaneous" interest by bringing in a fascinating object related to the theme so children start asking questions on their own. Find a cat with a litter of kittens and you're off and running!
- See how many parts of your environment you can involve in presenting ideas related to a theme. Bring in dress-up clothes and props related to the theme and accessories for children to use with blocks and in sand and water play. Find songs and games about the topic. Collect pictures and objects related to the theme that children can talk about. Sometimes you can find puzzles that depict some aspect of the theme, or make your own puzzles.
- Keep the theme going as long as children seem interested in it, bringing in new things to extend the topic.
- Even when you go on to other themes, or interest dies down, keep "remnants" of the theme around—a few pictures and props—so children remember and build upon what they learned.

Don't:

- Don't plan art projects to reflect a theme. Creative experiences should always be left "open-ended," exploring the materials and processes, rather than leading to a final product that looks like something.
- Don't force a theme if there is no interest or comprehension on the part of the children, but don't cut a theme off if children are still interested, just because a certain time period has passed.

Develop a "Thing Curriculum"

Children this age are fascinated by objects of all kinds. One valid curriculum approach would be to bring in a different object each day—all year long—for children to examine and talk about.

COLLECT MANY EXAMPLES OF A CERTAIN TYPE OF THING

Develop a collection of a particular type of common object, such as brushes. Start by bringing in a familiar sample, such as a hairbrush. Let the children talk about it and use it to brush dolls' hair or your hair. Ask them what other kinds of brushes they can think of. Each day bring in a different kind of brush—a tooth brush, a house painting brush, a make-up brush, a scrub brush, a pet grooming brush, a dish brush, etc. Talk about and demonstrate what each one is used for, as well as its characteristics. Keep your collection in a special box and let the children compare the brushes and watch the collection grow from day to day.

This "collection" approach broadens children's understanding of concepts, starting with the familiar. At the beginning they may have had one image of "brush." When you finish presenting many kinds of brushes, they have a much broader idea of what a brush is and the many possible functions and physical characteristics. You will have many meaningful, concrete opportunities to increase children's descriptive vocabulary as well.

Think of other such collections to make. Possibilities are really endless: things to make a mark with; boxes; sponges; balls; shoes . . . what else can you think of?

The Skills Approach

Some programs organize their planned activities around teaching children skills typical of their developmental level. The major fallacy that sometimes exists in this type of program planning is that you cannot "teach" a developmental skill, just as you cannot teach children to grow taller. Abilities such as walking up stairs alternating feet, cutting with scissors and speaking in full sentences develop naturally, "from within the child," when the child is ready, has had adequate preparatory experiences, and has opportunities to practice the skill.

However this approach is fine, as long as it is based on strong observations of children and what they are *already doing*. Then, giving children many opportunities to *practice* their new skills, sometimes with greater complexity or difficulty, strengthens their abilities. If teachers have a knowledge of basic child development and know which skills are likely to "come next," they can have materials available for the child to "drift over to" on her own, so that the skill can emerge.

The strength of this approach is that children are most often intensely interested in practicing whatever new skills they have mastered. If adults "meet the match" the children will have great fun and feel proud.

The danger is that possibly over-zealous parents and teachers, without meaning to, may frustrate children by offering activities that are too difficult, trying to get the child to advance faster. There might also be the tendency to compare children to each other, rather than the child to himself.

Develop a File of Your Own Favorite, "Tried and True" Activities

As you try activities in this and other resource books with your own group of children, some will be very successful, and others will fall flat. You will also create your own variations and entirely new activities. Develop a file of your favorite activities. You might organize them under the following categories: art projects; language development; cooking; sensory play; music; dramatic play; fine motor; gross motor.

Write out each activity on an index card. (Or, you might prefer to write the activity on notebook paper, and keep your file in a three-ring notebook.) List the materials you will need to gather ahead of time and the procedure for the project. Make notes to yourself on the vocabulary and concepts to emphasize when you present it. Also note which children particularly enjoyed the activity; which children had no interest; what to do differently next time.

Your personal project file can be useful when you are planning activities for the week ahead, helping you remember successes of the past. (Remember, children like repetition of the familiar.) You can also copy these activities to share with parents.

KEEP "ANECDOTAL RECORDS" ON CHILDREN

The best way to make sure your curriculum is right for all the children in your group is to know them well and observe how they respond. In numerous places in this book, you are advised to keep records of children's progress. You need a system for doing this. Get a three-ring binder, and put a divider in it for each child (or have a separate file folder for each one). Then on a piece of paper in that child's section, write down some pertinent information about him—his birthday, any special conditions to be aware of, the parents' name and phone numbers.

Start by writing an initial description of the child. It only has to be a paragraph or two. How did he behave on his first day in your program? Any special information or instructions from the parent? You might include a photograph and physical description of the child as well as how he responded to you and other children, his apparent language level, etc.

As time goes on, add notes when the child does things that seem to be significant. Record new accomplishments, such as a new motor skill (learning to pedal a tricycle), a new social skill (asking another child for a desired toy), or when he particularly enjoys an activity. Also record problems that arise, (when he hits or bites another child), or if he seems tired, listless, tense or angry. Behaviors such as this may seem insignificant at the time, but you may see a pattern emerge.

How to get this all done in your busy day? Many teachers carry around a small spiral notebook and a pencil and make a quick note during the day when they see something, transcribing it later during naptime in the child's file. Another good idea is to consciously observe one particular child each day. Notice where he chooses to play, with whom he plays, how he is talking, what he seems to be enjoying the most, what causes him difficulty, etc. Take little notes all day, and write them up into a paragraph later. If you do this consistently, then each child will get this more in-depth observation at least every two weeks.

This note-taking process not only makes you more conscious of each child's individuality and uniqueness, but also makes your job more rewarding because you are more likely to notice children's progress. The notes will come in handy as you plan curriculum activities, meet with other staff or parents to solve problems, and meet with parents periodically to discuss the child's progress.

RESOURCES

Bredecamp, Susan, *Developmentally Appropriate Practice.* NAEYC, Washington, D.C. 1987.
  In its description of appropriate ways to teach young children, this essential resource will get you thinking about what you are doing and why.

Miller, Karen, *Ages and Stages*. TelShare Publishing, Chelsea, MA. 1985.

You will find easy to follow descriptions of developmental stages of children from birth to age eight, along with many sample activities to reinforce new skills.

Miller, Karen, *The Outside Play and Learning Book*. Gryphon House Inc., Mt. Rainier, MD. 1989.

This book offers many possible activities, as well as planning strategies, for outside play, with a separate chapter for infants and toddlers as well as age-designated activities throughout the book.

CHAPTER 13

The Framework of Routines

The daily schedule in your program, the order of every-day events and the time allotted to them, forms the "framework" for your curriculum. Everything you do must be fit into this framework. Take the time to develop a schedule that works for you.

WHAT MAKES A GOOD DAILY SCHEDULE?

Consistency

Children do not know how long five minutes or an hour is. But they can remember the *sequence* of events. It is helpful to do the same segments of your routine in the same order every day. This gives children a sense of security—the feeling that the world is a dependable place. About five minutes before a change in the routine, the adult can talk about what is going to happen next. If children know what to expect, they are more likely to start preparing on their own.

Rituals

Toddlers and twos love "rituals"—doing the same actions, chants, songs, etc. at certain times of the day. Again, this has to do with feeling that the world is predictable, and that they "know the ropes." Have a special "good-morning" song or chant; a clean-up time song; a regular sequence of puppet, story, lullabies at naptime, etc. These give children a familiar "framework" for the day that helps them mark the passage of time.

Relaxed Pace

Anyone who has worked with children this age realizes that you cannot rush a toddler. If you try you might get all-out rebellion—a tantrum, or the "dishrag syndrome" when a child just falls on the floor and does nothing. If you remember that children learn as much participating in your daily routines as they do in the so-called "learning" segments of your program, it will be easier to allot an extra five minutes for handwashing, cleaning up, etc.

No Waiting

Do not line toddlers up and expect them to wait until everybody else is ready. This is close to torture for this active age (and isn't appropriate for any preschool children). Instead, as children are ready, allow them to go on to the next thing. For instance, have one caregiver go outside with children who are ready while another caregiver helps children inside finish up. If you work alone, have something for children to *do* while they wait, like play with miniature animals, or look at books.

Different Activity Levels

Offer a variety of different things to do, including active, physical activities and quiet, restful activities. Toddlers and twos are quite individual in their typical activity level and it can vary from day to day. By letting children make their own choices for large portions of the day, and by having a variety to guide them to when they seem either too wound up to sit still, or too tired for active play, you can meet individual needs of children and reduce the potential for conflict.

HINTS FOR PARTICULAR SEGMENTS OF THE DAY

Early Morning Greetings

Early morning is perhaps the most important time for comforting rituals and consistent routine. This is an important transition for the child. Any changes in the routine can be upsetting.

- Greet each child and parent warmly upon arrival. See if you can get other children to greet their arriving friends by name as well. This creates a feeling of friendship and belonging.
- Have some interesting materials set out for children to play with. A few choices might be easier to deal with than a whole room of things to choose from. "We have some nice, warm play-dough over there that we just made. Remember the books we read yesterday? They are over at that table. Or maybe you want to play with the dolls in the housekeeping corner this morning—they are just waking up."

Free Play Time

- Free-play time, or "free choice" time is when you allow children to play anywhere they wish in the room. This should be the longest sement of your day. Toddlers learn the most and are happiest when they can choose their own activities.
- Make sure there are plenty of interesting play choices, including familiar favorite toys and newer props. It helps to have at least two of some of the more popular toys to reduce fights and promote parallel play.
- Work together with other staff to decide who will do what during this time. One good system is to have a "focus person" and an "over-seer" person during play time. The focus person is the

one who may present a special project to a few children, or settle down to play with a particular child. The "over-seer" is in charge of watching the whole room, being alert to any dangerous situation arising, helping children settle disputes, changing a diaper, or helping a wandering child to settle.

- Maintain an awareness of the whole group, especially if you are the only adult with a group of children. As you play with children, remember to keep an ear open as well as the eyes on the back of your head, so you will know when your help is needed.

- Get the children's input on what they would like to do. For instance, you might ask them, "Shall I put out the crayons, or would you rather play with playdough this morning?" "Puzzles? Sure, we can get the puzzles out." Of course, you will have certain things planned, but it is good to make the children feel that they have some control as well.

- Have a couple of activities in mind to add when things start to lag and children seem bored or too many disputes arise. For instance, you might decide to wait until half way through the free play time to uncover the cornmeal table, or bring out a special set of blocks. The "novelty factor" will attract children to the activity, and give them a "fresh start."

Adult-Directed Activities During Free Play Time

There are many valid and fun learning activities for young children that require teacher supervision and participation. Messy art projects, cooking, examining objects that might be dangerous to just leave out, are a few examples.

- Entice instead of requiring participation. Use the "flop and do" technique. Instead of calling children together for the activity, simply "flop" down on the floor and start doing the activity, or set up the project and wait for your first "takers." Children who are interested will be drawn over to it.
- Keep the group size small. If more than two or three other children participate, a toddler will find it difficult to pay attention to you, and will be distracted by the other children. (Have interesting alternative activities available for "waiters," as well as the rich free-choice environment of your classroom.) A small group size lets you converse with children as individuals, allowing them to express themselves as well as listen. You will have a greater idea if concepts are "sinking in." This allows for more active, hands-on participation on the part of children and will simplify your clean-up as well.
- Make sure children who want one, get a turn. It's true that children tend to crowd around when a new, interesting activity is offered, but when they learn that they will, indeed, get a turn, they will come to trust you and do something else in the meantime.
- Allow children *not* to participate. If a child is very busy playing at your water table and would rather not cut up fruit, allow him to stay with his chosen activity. Trust children this age to go to what they need most in a well-enriched environment.

Circle Time

"Circle Time" or "Group Time" is when a small group of children sit down to participate in teacher-directed activities. There is good reason to question having circle time at all with toddlers. However, older two-year-olds may be able to enjoy a *short* but interesting small group time. Hints for success:

- Keep the group size small—5 or 6 children at the most. If necessary divide the children and sit down with a few, while someone else takes the others outside, or has a circle time with them somewhere else.

- Keep the time short—5 to 10 minutes. Don't hesitate to disband if they just don't seem "with-it" that day. You don't want children to dread this part of the day.

- Hold your circle time in the same place each day. A large area rug can define the space for children. Minimize distractions by sitting with your back to the wall, and have children facing you. Make sure everyone can see and participate. (Carpet samples placed on the floor for children to sit on help.)

- Make it okay for children to get up and move away if their attention span is not sufficient. Any child on a given day, may simply not be able to participate more than a few minutes.

- Invent a gathering chant, such as "Come to the circle, come to the circle, come to the circle . . . we'll have a little fun."

- Have a greeting ritual. Your puppet might come out and sing each child's name. It is important to acknowledge each child by saying his name and perhaps giving him a touch.

- Try to keep your "sequence" of circle time events the same from day to day. For instance, first a puppet greeting. Then a particular fingerplay; then show them an object from your surprise bag; then a movement activity; then a short story; then a closing chant or ritual.

- Set a special tone for your circle time. Make it pleasant, accepting, comfortable, with an undercurrent of anticipation.

Clean-up Time

It's well known that toddlers like dumping more than they like filling, but remember that they also like interacting with an adult, imitating, and sticking things in holes.

- Have a special place for everything. If there is a picture label on the shelf for many of the toys, and things are kept in the same place every day, children can feel a sense of control of their environment when they put things away in just the right spot. It can have the feel of a fun matching game.
- Have a good reason for cleaning up. "As soon as the toys are all put away, we can go outside, (or eat our snack)." Since children *love* to play outside and eat, they will be more motivated to help.
- Use clean-up time for a simple sorting game. Have children put all the toys on the floor into a laundry basket. Then take one out at a time and say, "Where does this go?" If you have several distinct areas of your room—housekeeping, blocks, and table toys, for instance, then children are classifying toys as they show you where they go (and put them away).
- Create storage boxes with holes in the lids. For toys with lots of little pieces, like beads to string, crayons, fit together manipulatives and pegs, find a storage container with a lid, such as a shoebox or a large coffee can. Cut a hole in the lid that the child can drop the pieces through. Toddlers love to stick things in holes, so this will entice their participation.
- Make clean-up time a pleasant, social activity. Describe what individuals are doing to help. Sing a pleasant clean-up song. Be lavish with the thank-you's. Be sure to congratulate the group for a job well done. Look around the room with the children and comment on how nice it looks and how everyone helped.

Going Outside

Energetic toddlers and two-year-olds love going outside, and really need outdoor play.

- Putting on outer clothes in cold weather can be time consuming. If possible, have one staff person go outside to receive those who are ready, so children will not have to wait.
- Have a toileting/diaper-changing time before you go outside, perhaps at very end of free play time, so you will not have to bring a child inside, leaving behind an unsafe child/staff ratio.
- Plan some special optional activities for your outside play time, just as you do for your inside time. It could be an art activity

such as painting with water, some special toys for the sandbox, a circle game, a box of balls, etc. As well as enhancing your learning program, you will reduce boredom and conflict.

- Have an outside clean-up time. Before you go back inside, the children can help you collect sand toys, balls and other materials. They can "drive" riding toys into a shed and even sweep the sidewalks with a small broom.
- If there are at least two staff people, you can have a few children at a time go inside and begin the diapering/toileting routine. This may reduce the waiting time.

Lunchtime/Snacktime

Food has all sorts of emotional overtones. Snack time and lunch time should always be pleasant, relaxed, and social.

- Make handwashing an essential ritual before lunch and snack times.
- Don't bring children to the table until the food is in the room and children can begin to eat.
- Let children help set the table and hand out napkins.
- Bibs are a good idea. There are bibs made of small terry towels with rib-knit neck openings that children can put on themselves, giving them a greater feeling of independence.

- Try serving "family style." Instead of simply dishing out the food, or having it on plates already when children sit down, "introduce" each food and let them tell you "a lot" or "a little" as you dish it out in front of them. "Today we have yummy meatloaf, broccoli that looks like trees, and fluffy, white mashed potatoes. Mark, how much meatloaf would you like? Broccoli? Potatoes?" You are building vocabulary as you name and describe foods as well as talk about quantity.

- Encourage children to try a little of everything, but do not pressure them to eat everything on their plates. Parents are often amazed that children will eat things that they refuse at home. They are copying their teacher and their friends.

- Sit down and eat with the children. You can model good table manners, without overtly stressing them with children. You can talk positively about the meal, as well as simply guiding pleasant conversation about other topics.

- Minimize spills by finding cups with large stable bases, and not filling them too full. When a spill occurs, have the child clean it up himself using a sponge you keep handy.

- Even toddlers can help clean up by scraping their own dishes into a large receptacle when they are through eating and putting their silverware into a bucket of soapy water. It might be quicker and neater to do it yourself but it is good to give children this responsibility.

- Do not require children to stay seated at the table until everyone is finished. If there is another adult, that person can supervise bathroom and handwashing activities as well as diapering in preparation for naptime.

PLACE SETTINGS

This encourages children to replace their cups on the cup circles, well away from the edge of the table, rather than right on the edge as is common for toddlers, reducing spills.

Materials:

Colored construction paper   *Clear self-adhesive vinyl*
Scissors

Create a "place setting" with construction paper outlines of a plate, a smaller circle for a cup at the upper right of the plate outline, and a spoon. Cover with clear contact paper. Setting the table thus becomes a matching game.

Rest Time

Most toddlers and two year olds still very much need a naptime in which to "recharge their batteries" after an active morning of play. The hardest thing about rest time can be getting children from the lunch table to their cots or rest mats without chaos. There is much that must happen during this interval. Lunch dishes must be stacked and returned to the kitchen, the tables wiped, and the floor swept. Children must have diapers changed or go to the toilet, both with subsequent handwashing. Then children must be settled comfortably on their cots and "tucked in." Going to sleep is another "emotion laden" time of the day when children are most likely to miss "Mommy."

- Assign staff roles. Who will clean up lunch? Who will put out cots or rest mats? Who will supervise toileting? Who will diaper children? Who will tuck children in and get them settled down? These and other duties can be rotated from day to day, but it is good to know who will do what on a given day.

- Anticipate nap time pleasantly. Never talk about it in a negative way. During lunch you can say, "Ah . . . soon we will be able to lie down and snuggle into our blankets and have a nice rest."

- Start calming down early. At lunch, and during the transition, start talking quietly. Put calm music on. Dim the lights when everyone has finished eating.

- Place children's cots or rest mats in the same place each day. This allows them to drift off to sleep with a better sense of security. Label cots or mats with the child's name. Make a chart to help you and other staff remember. Place cots as far apart as possible to limit disturbances from other children and minimize the spread of airborne germs.

- If children must wait to have their diapers changed or use the bathroom after lunch, plan some non-messy, quiet activities for them to do while they wait. A cornmeal table, or books are two possibilities.

- Try having a short story time after lunch. While one adult reads to children, the other adult puts out cots and cleans up. You might collect special naptime stories and books about sleeping.

- Allow children to have at naptime their special security toys such as their own personal stuffed animal or security blanket.

- Sing children individual lullabies with their names in them as you go around and tuck them in. It makes each child feel special.

- Give children a calming back rub when you tuck them in.

- Remember that children must never be left unsupervised, even while they are sleeping. Use this time to relax a bit yourself as well as do some planning or professional reading.

- If you have children who do not fall asleep after about a half hour (rare with this age group) allow them to get up and engage in quiet activities such as playing with playdough, looking at books, or listening to stories with earphones. It is ideal to have a separate room or a space separated from the nappers with a divider to minimize noise distraction because it is hard for children to remember to be quiet.

A YAWNING PUPPET

Materials:

Puppet with a mouth that opens and closes

This puppet could be a "specialist" who only comes out right before naptime to sing to children softly, and talk to them, yawning all the while. Yawns are very catching!

The After-nap Transition

When children wake up from their naps, they should be greeted into the waking world gently by loving teachers with a smile and a hug. Children will need to use the bathroom or have their diapers changed, and wash their hands. Cots or mats must be put away.

- Children need something to do while the caregiver is occupied with these routines. Several tables can be set up with easy activities. Puzzles and manipulatives, books, and playdough are good choices.

- Allow children to wake up slowly and pleasantly. Have something the children who wake up early can do. Don't force them to remain on their cots.

- If you must wake some sound sleepers to get on with the rest of the day, try to do so gently. Turn the lights on and supervise the other children in their bathroom and handwashing activities. If the normal commotion of the room doesn't wake them up, get them up yourself and allow them to "come to" slowly with quiet activities. Parents often object to letting children take overly long naps, because they stay awake too late at night.

Afternoon

It seems that in many programs, the morning is fine, but the afternoon tends to be "loose" with more random behavior and "chaos" on the part of children. Sometimes this is because there is a change of staff, and less trained, part-time staff take over. It could be because the staff is tired, or the children are bored. Usually a little planning is all that is needed to make the afternoon just as interesting and enjoyable as the morning.

- The afternoons should contain all the time elements of the morning, just condensed a little bit, because there is less time. There will be snack time, indoor play time, outdoor play time, and possibly another short circle time. Special activities should be planned to enliven the play times.

- Try to plan something different. If painting was an activity in the morning, offer a different color of paint in the afternoon. Perhaps put out some different puzzles or manipulatives. If you had the water table out in the morning, tubs of rice would be fun to play with in the afternoon.

- An extra juice snack late in the day can reduce crankiness and make everyone feel better.
- Plan for choices of non-messy, calming, "winding down" activities late in the day, rather than vigorous, boisterous activities. Have a general clean-up time about a half hour before the end of the day. Singing, stories, puzzles, playdough, table blocks are possible late-day options.

Moving from One Place to Another

If you have to move children from one place to another, (go down a hall, move to a different room), use the opportunity for some creative movement.

- Children love to play "train." Have them hold on to the shoulders of the child in front of them and make chugging and whistling sounds as they move along.
- Challenge children to move in different ways as they go to the new place. "Everybody tip-toe and see how quiet we can be." "Let's take big giant-steps to the exercise room."

Going Home Time

This can be a hard time of the day for children. Not only are they sometimes tired, they are more likely to miss their parents when they start to see their friends going home. It makes sense to do all you can to make children feel comfortable.

- Greet each parent warmly, by name. If you have not met the individual who is picking up the child, do not be embarrassed to ask for identification. Check to see if the center has been notified that this person was coming, or if that person's name is on the enrollment form. If not, do not release the child until you have contacted the parent.

- Take time to relate some positive things about the child's day to the parent. Have his things together and ready to go. Although problems certainly should not be hidden from parents, it is not advisable to confront them with a litany of complaints at the end of the day when they are rushed and tired. Plan to meet at a time when it is easier to talk. (See Discipline chapter.)

- Use time with late children for special attention. Perhaps save some extra special toy for that time. Let the child help you "close down the room," with the routine things you do each day. Sweeping. Putting water in the guinea pig's bottle. This is a good time for one-on-one conversations.

- As children leave, give them a hug, a smile, and tell them you are looking forward to the next time they are there so you can have more fun together.

MAKE A DISPLAY OF YOUR DAILY ROUTINE IN PHOTOGRAPHS

Photograph each separate segment of your daily routine and create a bulletin board from these photographs. This can serve two purposes:

- *Parent Awareness.* As new parents consider enrolling in your program they can get an immediate impression of what goes on during the day. It gives you an opportunity to talk to parents about what you do, how the children develop independence, how much time they spend playing, your lunch and nap routines, etc.

- *Child Awareness.* Children will love looking at the pictures on this display. You can ask them, "What are we doing here?" "What happens next?" "Who is that . . . what is he doing?" During the day you can take individual children over to the display and ask them which picture represents what is going on at that point. This symbolic representation (photo) of real occurrences is also a good pre-reading activity. Children will become more conscious of what they do each day and realize that they are an important part of the group.

CHAPTER 14

Guiding Children's Behavior

Did you open the book to this chapter first? Helping toddlers and two-year-olds learn to interact with others comfortably, to postpone gratification and to deal with temporary frustration is one of the greatest challenges of working with this age. You will spend much energy interpreting children to each other, arranging your environment to minimize conflict and teaching children more effective ways to get their needs met. This can be frustrating, especially when it gets in the way of your other plans. It helps if you can say to yourself, "THIS IS WHAT IT IS ALL ABOUT." Truly, learning to control their own behavior is one of the major and most important things children learn at this time in their development.

One problem caregivers have with discipline, is that they do not enjoy the process. Even when we know that children are

173

learning from a well-handled discipline situation, it does not seem like a rewarding thing to be doing. It's much more fun to admire a child's easel painting, or help them build their first block tower. Yet, what they learn from well-handled discipline has much longer effects, and even greater implications for their abilities to succeed in school and life later on. Good behavior patterns are learned gradually, through repeated experiences. REGARD YOURSELF AS A COACH.

Help yourself find gratification in this aspect of your work by keeping good anecdotal records of children's behaviors. It will be easier to notice that Sarah is only having one tantrum a week now, whereas several months ago, she was having three tantrums a day. You will see that Nicole, who clung to your leg the whole first month, is now holding her own with other children in the group. You are more likely to regard Justin's name calling as progress when you realize that several months ago, all he could think of to do was hit children when he didn't get his way.

Back to our question, "Did you turn to this chapter first?" If you did, go back and at least skim the rest of the book, and then promise to read it in detail later. Behavior does not happen in isolation. There are no quick and easy "cookbook" answers to discipline problems. Everything is related. When you find a well-functioning classroom of toddlers and two-year-olds, you will find a well-planned environment with ample equipment, a program where children have many choices of interesting activities, a teacher who encourages talking and language development, a program where parents and staff have good communications, and most of all, a teacher who understands these children—knows what to expect and what not to expect from them, who is loving, flexible, and "tuned-in" to the little individuals around her.

STRUCTURE FOR SUCCESS—30 PREVENTIVE DISCIPLINE TECHNIQUES

There is much that you can do to cut down on behavior problems in the first place. Of course, not all of these things will work all of the time, but used consistently, they can go a long way toward building a more peaceful classroom.

Caregiver Style

1. *Get in touch.* Touch each child within a few minutes of seeing each other each day. Go over to them. Say their name. Make eye-contact. Smile. A hand on the shoulder, a pat on the head. This makes children feel "counted," or acknowledged. They will feel less compelled to "act out" to get noticed.

2. *Model gentleness.* Speak to children in a gentle tone of voice. Show concern and comfort children who are hurt. Children will imitate your mode of interaction.

3. *Get down on the child's eye level when you talk to him.* You need to be sure that you have the child's attention before you can expect him to follow your instructions. Make eye contact.

4. *Get close.* Move near to children when you want to talk to them or intervene rather than calling across the room or the playground. The close presence of an adult in itself can prevent problems from arising.

5. *State things positively.* Instead of saying "Don't pull Jennier's hair," say, "Touch Jennifer's hair gently." Early language learners may only focus on the last words you say, so they will remember ". . . pull Jennifer's hair." Negatives are harder to understand. Always state what you *do* want the child to do.

6. *Play with children.* Fewer behavior problems arise when there is active play involvement by the adult. Get down on the floor with children and watch with interest as they play. By playing with them, you are helping them do interesting things with the materials rather than just taking them from other children and building up their hoard.

7. *Praise positive behaviors.* Be sure to notice and comment when children demonstrate they have learned better ways to interact. "Good talking, Bruce! You told Ashley that was your chair, and he went and got another one."

Environment

8. *Make your environment as "allowable" as possible.* See the Safety chapter to eliminate all possible safety hazards. Put

up fragile or valuable items you don't want children to handle. Block off areas of the environment where you don't want children to be. You will spend less time prohibiting and frustrating children.

9. *Have enough materials*. Have duplicates of popular toys and many of such things as sand buckets and shovels so children don't have to fight for favorites.

10. *Arrange the room to minimize conflict*. Divide your room into several smaller spaces. Shelves and low dividers can be arranged to make small spaces where children can play, less distracted by other children.

11. *Avoid crowding*. If too many children are forced to play in a small space, more aggression will arise over toys as well as play space. Try moving furniture to create slightly larger spaces; or divide the space to encourage the children to play in different areas of the room.

Organization and Routines

12. *Supervise closely*. Children are less likely to hurt each other if an adult is close at hand. If at least two adults are working with a group, try to have one adult be the "play supervisor" while the other adult takes care of custodial matters such as diapering.

13. *Minimize waiting*. Don't bring children to the lunch table until the food is there. Have one adult go outside to receive children as they are ready, rather than expecting them to line up and wait. Use fingerplays, games like "Can You Do What I Do?" or show children pictures when a wait is unavoidable.

14. *Allow enough time*. When adults are in a hurry and pressure children to go faster, they naturally slow down. If they are overwhelmed by the rush, they may collapse and refuse to move. It's best to take your time and let children enjoy the routines, gently moving them along if time is becoming important.

15. *Provide numerous activity choices*. There should be more than one thing to do. It is important for toddlers in this autonomy stage of their development to be able to make decisions about what they want to play with. If there are many interesting

toys and activities available, it will be easier to wait for a desired toy someone else is using.

16. *Don't over-structure.* Avoid too much large group activity such as circle time or teacher-led activities where all children are expected to do the same thing at the same time. (Remember that eating is one such activity . . . not to be cut short.) Too much large group activity may cause them to become restless and uncooperative.

17. *Set consistent limits.* Don't prohibit children from climbing on the tables one day and allow it or ignore it the next day. Have a set of rules that are consistent. Rules should be as few as possible and limited to protecting the children's safety, as in not climbing on furniture, and not hurting each other. Make sure all staff are aware of the classroom rules so they can be enforced consistently by all adults.

18. *Develop rituals to encourage cooperation.* Toddlers often resist doing something if someone tells them to do it . . . just out of principle. If you signal various aspects of your routine such as cleaning up, washing hands, coming to the circle time, getting ready to go inside, etc. with songs and chants, this is a "signal" a child can read. They are more likely to do what the song or chant suggests because it is their way of showing that they "know the ropes." Give children advance warning, before your ritual begins, of changes in the routine. "We'll be going inside soon."

19. *Remain flexible—go with the flow.* Are children truly enjoying themselves on a glorious day outside? Extend your time. No interest in your planned art activity? Put it aside for another day.

20. *Allow children not to participate.* Instead of *requiring* that all children sit down to do your planned activity, *invite* one or two children to join you. If they decline your invitation and want to play elsewhere, that's okay. Let them have some control.

21. *Provide plenty of outside time.* When the weather permits, outside play allows children to be their natural, active selves. They will be less tense and more ready for quiet activities indoors when they have had ample time outdoors.

22. *Provide active play indoors.* Toddlers can't wait until they

are outside to climb and be active. An indoor slide or small climber helps. Also have a number of active games to play with children. Or dance to music. This provides an acceptable release of tension.

Child to Child: As Situations Happen

23. *Catch it on the build.* Head them off at the pass! When you notice tension building into a major conflict, coach children to use the words or actions they need to deal with the situation peacefully.

24. *Teach a gentle touch.* Young children are sometimes rough in their interactions—they push, grab, pull. Show them how to touch each other gently, without hurting. The phrase, "gentle hands" or "friendly hands" may remind children to moderate their actions.

25. *Train children to ask for things they want.* "May I play with that?" is more likely to elicit cooperation than simply grabbing a toy. It is also good to train the child who has the wanted object to say, "In a minute," if he is not ready to give it up right away. (See sharing section of Social chapter.)

26. *Interpret children to each other.* Non-verbal toddlers often respond with a cry or hard to understand words of protest. Help the perpetrator understand the effect of his actions. Give alternatives. "Melissa's sitting there right now. She doesn't want you to push her off the chair. Come sit with me."

27. *Wait!* "Wait" is a good word to stop aggression. If you are on the other side of the room and see Chrissy about to slug Jeremy, call out, "Chrissy . . . wait!" She is more likely to pause to see what you want than obey if you shouted "Stop," or "Don't do that."

28. *Teach assertiveness against aggression.* Teach children to use simple phrases such as "Stop that," "I don't like that," when another child is threatening them or bothering them.

29. *Redirect children to acceptable activities.* If a child is doing something not allowed, such as climbing on the table, redirect the child to the closest possible allowable thing. "Oh, Tiffany . . . I see you want to climb. But the tables are not for climbing.

Let's go over here to the steps." "Pegs are not for throwing,
Adam. Here there are some yarn balls you can throw."

30. *Stay close to trouble makers.* Keep a special eye on a child
who is known to bite or hurt others frequently. Stay as close
as possible. Perhaps assign a volunteer or extra staff person
to stick right with the child and help him or her interact appropriately.

STRATEGIES FOR HANDLING AGGRESSION

One of the main things toddlers must learn is not to hurt their
fellow man. True, some children are more aggressive than others,
but almost all toddlers may, at one time or another, resort to
hurting behaviors as a quick "means to an end." Most hurting
behaviors that occur with toddlers in groups have to do with "the
territorial imperative"—fighting over toys or space, or the attention of an adult. On rare occasions, a child will hurt another child
simply to "get some action going." Sometimes hurting is a defensive
gesture to another aggressor—literally, "beating him to the
punch." It is the caregiver's role to teach the child an acceptable
alternative.

The acceptable alternative, unfortunately, is one that is very
difficult for toddlers—"talking it over." Toddlers don't yet have
the necessary language skills to get out some complex ideas . . .
let alone in a time of stress. Furthermore, toddlers don't have
the reasoning ability—the flexible thinking necessary for higher-
level problem solving. They are not very practiced at considering
the other guy's point of view either.

Remember, that children who hurt others need special attention
from you. While they need you to teach them different ways to
handle their frustration, they very much need to know that you
still love them. It is their *behavior* you don't approve of, not them.
If they feel rejected by you, their negative behavior may even
increase, because they may give up trying to win your approval.

TEN STEP METHOD FOR HANDLING AGGRESSION

1. *Have a rule, "no hurting."* Group all hurting behaviors together, including pinching, hair pulling, scratching, hitting,
pushing, kicking and biting. (Biting will be considered sepa-

rately, below.) Your rule to children will be "no hurting." Otherwise, if you have a rule of no scratching, for instance, children will soon think of other ways to hurt.

2. *Stop the hurting behavior as soon as you see it happen.* If the child does not respond to verbal cues from you, physically separate the children yourself. Do not ignore hurting behavior, because toddlers may take that to mean that the behavior is okay with you, or even that you approve of it.

   Likewise, don't allow the child to hurt you. If the child hits, kicks or bites you, do not ignore it or make light of it . . . even if it didn't hurt. Tell the child that that is not allowed and you don't like it. Be serious. It is scary for a child to be able to hurt an adult.

3. *Be serious in voice tone (without shouting), facial expression, and body language.* Get down, eye to eye with the aggressor, and hold her arms or shoulders to keep her attention. Make it clear that you do not like it and will not allow it. "You hurt Brandy. Scratching people is not okay. I won't let you hurt people." Add, ". . . and I will not let people hurt you." This conveys a message of "fairness," and helps children feel safe.

4. *Point out how the victim feels.* "Look, Brandy is crying because that hurt him. See the red marks on his arm?" It is important that toddlers learn that other people "feel." They must learn the consequences of their action.

5. *Immediately turn your attention to the victim.* Comfort the victim in front of the aggressor. "I'm sorry you got hurt, Brandy. Let's see what we can do to make you feel better." Sometimes it helps get the message across if you have the aggressor help with the comforting, such as getting some ice or a cool wash cloth to put on the scratch. But be careful. Don't let this become a way for the aggressor to get some extra attention from you.

6. *Separate the aggressor from other children, briefly.* (This does not mean you should set up a "time out" chair. A time out chair has only limited effectiveness with toddlers because they won't sit on it very long. Also, some teachers treat it like a "dunce chair" and use it to humiliate the child, which is DEFINITELY not the purpose.) Simply bring the child to another

part of the room away from the others. The reasons to separate the child are 1) to allow her some time to calm down and think about what just happened, and 2) to communicate the message that she will miss the fun of playing with others if she hurts people. A few minutes is adequate.

7. *Talk to the aggressor.* 1) Start by acknowledging the child's motivating feeling. 2) Restate that the hurting behavior is not allowed. 3) *Then talk about what to do next time.* Depending on the situation, you can talk to the child while the children are still together, or when she has been separated from the others. "I know you were upset because you wanted the red truck and Max wouldn't give it to you. But it's not okay to hit Max. Next time you want something, ask your friend for it. Say, 'Max, can I play with that truck with you?'" Offer this advice in a helpful tone, like a coach. But be careful not to give the child too much attention. You don't want her to act up just to get some one-on-one attention from you. Leave her and go about your normal activities (be sure you can still see the child).

8. *Ease the reentry.* In a minute or two allow the child to reenter the group by asking, "Are you ready to play with the other kids again?" If possible, involve her in something totally different from the activity that caused the conflict, and with another child. Tactile play—playdough, water, sand—is often a good choice because it is soothing and open-ended.

9. *Record the incident.* Make a quick note of what happened in the child's anecdotal records, while it is fresh in your memory. Record the time of day, the other children involved, what the child did, what you did and how he responded. These details can be very useful later in analyzing his behavior and working with parents and other staff to develop strategies for dealing with him.

10. *Catch the child doing something right.* As soon as possible after the child has reentered the group, give him some positive attention, including a touch like a pat on the shoulder, for some positive behavior, whether it is commenting on how he is stacking some blocks, how he is helping you set the table, or a generous act like giving another child a book. You need to quickly reestablish your friendship with the child and rees-

tablish his self-image as a capable, likeable person, rather than dwelling on the negative aggressive actions.

DEALING WITH BITING

Biting is such a severe and serious hurting behavior the topic needs some special attention. Biting should be treated in the same way as other hurting behaviors described above in the "Ten-Step Method for Handling Aggression." Try all of those strategies, repeatedly and consistently before you give up.

If you have a lot of biting in your program, take a good, hard look at your set up and what you are doing and see if there are some factors that are contributing to it. Go back and reread the "30 Preventive Discipline Techniques" section. Not enough toys, over-crowding, inadequate adult attention are often contributing factors. Keep a journal. Record any changes you make and if they seem to help.

In all fairness, though, sometimes everything is just fine in a program and children still bite. Biting does occur in high quality programs, but usually with less frequency. Sometimes you will go along for months with no biting incidents, and then, suddenly there is a "rash" of biting, often stimulated by one child.

Try to figure out what is causing the biting. Realize that children biting other children is *rarely* caused by teething pain. There are plenty of other things to chomp down on besides your friend's arm. If you think teething is the cause, make sure the child has plenty of other things to chew on. A clean, wet wash rag that has been frozen in the freezer is one idea, or keep a supply of raw carrot sticks around. Most biting is "instrumental aggression," fighting over toys, space or attention.

Some programs report that "victim training" helps. Teach other children to shout, "No biting!" when a biter approaches in a menacing way. Help the potential victim remember this by saying it with them if you are near-by. This often takes potential biters by surprise and stops them in their tracks.

The preventive technique that works best is #30—"Stay close to trouble makers." Before you say it is impossible when you have a whole group to watch, give it a try. As much as possible, position yourself, or another staff person, close to your biter during the normal routines of the day, and especially during free-play time. You might decide to cut down, for the time being, on special activities that require your close supervision, such as fingerpainting, just so you can "hang close" to the child in question.

If necessary, see if you can get some extra short-term special assistance. Does your program have a "floater" staff person who might be able to help? Are there any community volunteers who occasionally serve your program? Maybe a parent of another child in your program could help out. Any "work/study" students available? Even a mature school-age child enrolled in your program might be able to help, with close guidance from you. Simply assign that person to stick right with your potential biter, play with the child, help the child negotiate, and generally "catch it on the build." Try to keep it subtle, so the child is not aware that he is getting this special attention because he is a threat to others. Often just a week or so of this special attention is all that is needed to break a bad habit and teach the child more acceptable ways to interact. If you stop biting behaviors quickly you are not allowing the child's negative self-image to grow.

Keep in mind that biting is a normal behavior of toddlers, even though not all children are biters. It is one thing that some children try. It is a behavior that needs to be dealt with quickly and consistently, but it does not necessarily indicate severe emotional problems. Biting usually disappears when the child gains language skill and learns to defend himself verbally. (Biting in children over four can indicate more serious emotional problems and may call for the special assistance of a psychologist.)

Do keep good records about bites. Fill out an accident report, recording all the details of the incident and describing the first aid administered. The wound should be cleaned with soap and water. Ice can help reduce the swelling and pain. If the skin is broken, it might need to be seen by a doctor. Parents should be called and informed of the incident. Better that they hear it from you with accurate information than be surprised when they pick the child up. Also tell the parents of the biter what happened and talk about strategies to stop the behavior.

Keep a "bite log" for your classroom, describing the date, time of day and children involved in any biting incidents. This may give you a clue. You may find that more biting occurs when children are tired or hungry, or when a new child has been added to the group.

DEALING WITH THE "DIFFICULT CHILD"—PROBLEM SOLVING WITH PARENTS

All toddlers can be "difficult" from time to time, but there is the occasional child who concerns you, either because of continuous aggressive behavior that doesn't change in spite of all your well-thought-out strategies, or one who causes you concern for other reasons. Before you label the child "emotionally disturbed," or expel her from your program, have a problem-solving session with her parents and any other staff who work directly with her. Emotions are likely to be running high, so proceed with your best professional behavior.

Before you call such a conference, keep careful notes for at least a week. When is the behavior occurring? Under what circumstances? Is it with one other particular child? How have you handled it? How did the child respond? When you come to the conference prepared in this way, it allows you to talk in specifics and describe actual happenings and behaviors rather than coming out with vague and sometimes judgmental statements, such as "Your child has been very aggressive."

First, have understanding for the parents. They are likely to be feeling frustrated, embarrassed, even threatened. When their child misbehaves, they feel it is a reflection on them and their skill as parents (even though they may not say this). Parents may blame themselves. "If I hadn't put her in child care she wouldn't be behaving this way." "If I earned more money, my wife wouldn't have to work and could stay home with the child." They may resent their child. "Why is she humiliating me this way? Why can't she behave like the other children?" They may even panic . . . "If she gets 'kicked out,' I'll lose my job, we won't be able to pay the rent . . ."

Parents may also blame your program. "She never behaved this way before." "She learned this behavior here . . . you are turning her into a monster." It may be true that the child never behaved that way at home. A group situation presents different problems to a child.

The important thing is not to assign blame. It is *not* always the parent's fault, any more than is the program always to blame. Put the parents at ease by thanking them for coming and being willing to help figure this out. Ask them for their *insights*. How do they assess the situation? What do they think might be causing it? What do they do at home when the child behaves this way? Do they have any suggestions for you? Reassure the parents that all children have problems from time to time. Working together, you can figure out how to help the child, so the behavior won't worsen, and he will learn more effective ways to behave. Most of all, the parents need to hear that you like their child and want to help, rather than figuring out how to punish him.

Together, work up a plan. Agree about what you will all do to try to prevent the behavior from happening again, and how all of you will react the next time, if the child does it again. Agree to keep notes and get together at a specified later date to talk about the progress. If your strategies work, it will allow you all to give yourselves a pat on the back. If the problem persists, you "go back to the drawing boards," and think of something else to do. Perhaps this is the time to bring in professional help for advice—a child psychologist or other helping professional in your community.

If all else fails, especially in the case of biting or other severe hurting behaviors, it sometimes helps to give the child a break from child care . . . a change of scene. Don't "kick the child out" or close the door completely. Suggest the parent keep the child out of the program for a month or so, perhaps finding temporary substitute care with a private sitter in the meantime, and try again later. The parent could bring the child back for occasional visits, in which the parent stays with him, to keep in touch, and keep the feelings of friendship alive. The child may come to miss interaction with friends and realize the consequences of his actions. Sometimes a month or two makes a big difference in a child's ability to adjust. And you are not abandoning him.

What do you say to the parent whose methods of discipline conflict with what you believe in? This most often involves the issue of physical punishment, and especially biting a child back.

- Put on your parent educator's hat. Point out how research shows that children's aggressive behavior usually increases when they are given physical punishment. They are imitating the behavior of important adults. If an adult hits or bites them, they reason that they should be able to bite other people to get their way.
- Tell the parent that by law, you are not allowed to administer

physical punishment of any kind, including biting back, spanking, slapping, shaking, or washing the child's mouth with soap or bitter mouthwash.

- Focus on the teaching or "coaching" nature of good discipline practices. You want to show the child *how* to act, not how *not* to act.
- Avoid coming right out and criticizing the parent. Instead suggest a way that is better for the overall development of the child. Take an "experimental" approach. "Let's try this and see what happens." Ask for their cooperation, because consistency between the home and the child care program is important.

Even if it takes a long time to conquer a particular problem, as long as you are all working on it together, it is easier to tolerate. Remember, the child is worth it. You *can* make a difference.

CAREGIVER BEHAVIORS TO AVOID

Before we end this chapter, it is important to talk about some methods that adults should *not* engage in. This list may be helpful in training new staff. Be sure you always talk about why, and what to do instead.

- Do not use physical punishment: no spanking, slapping hands, hitting with a ruler; no shaking (particularly dangerous!); no squeezing; no twisting arms or yanking; no washing out mouths.
- Do not threaten or scare children. Don't threaten, I'm going to tell your father (or mother). Instead, handle the situation yourself and confer with the parent as described above, without using this as a threat. Also, do not threaten physical punishment, even if you don't intend to follow through.
- Do not yell at children. This only frightens them and they will not hear your words.
- Do not isolate a child where he or she cannot be directly seen and supervised by an adult.
- Do not physically constrain or confine a child in any way, other than holding.
- Do not humiliate children. No name calling. Don't make the child sit in a certain place for "bad kids."

- Do not use negative adjectives about the child. Do not say, "You are a bad girl (or boy)," or call the child "mean," "disturbed," etc. Instead, focus on the behavior. "Hitting is not allowed. It hurts. I won't let you hurt anyone."

- Do not withhold food as a punishment, such as not allowing the child to eat dessert. This form of punishment in childhood may be the root of eating disorders later on.

- Do not force the child to apologize or kiss and make up. If it is forced, he will not mean it, and will only be learning to be hypocritical. Teachers have even observed children hitting another child and then immediately saying, "I'm sorry," as though that made it all right. Instead, focus on showing how it made the other child feel, and leave it at that.

- Do not ask children why they did it. They can't analyze their behavior that way, and would not be able to verbalize it anyway. Instead, give your interpretation. "I know you want that toy and it's hard to wait, but . . ."

- Do not ask them how they would feel if someone did that to them. ("How would you feel if someone threw sand in your eyes?") That sounds threatening, rather than building empathy.

- Do not use clinical labels when talking about a child—"hyperactive," "emotionally disturbed . . ." Instead, just deal with the behavior as it happens.

- Do not talk negatively about the child in front of the child or other children. This is a frequent error of busy teachers and parents, especially at drop off or pick up times. If you need to discuss something, suggest a phone call or short meeting. Remind yourselves that even not-yet-talking children can understand a great deal.

WRAP UP

Remember to regard each discipline situation as a learning opportunity. The motivation for children to behave acceptably is to have friends, enjoy the company of others, and gain the attention and approval of important adults. Like anything else, children can only learn when their self-esteem is intact. That's why this chapter is titled "guidance," rather than "punishment." Our goal is not only to get children's compliance in the immediate incident, but to give children strategies for functioning independently later on. Results are not immediate. The process can be disruptive and annoying. But remember, it is among the most important things you are doing, with the most long-ranging benefits for children.

RESOURCES

Crary, Elizabeth, *Kids Can Cooperate, A Practical Guide to Teaching Problem Solving*. Parenting Press, Inc., Seattle, WA 1984.

Mitchell, Grace, *A Very Practical Guide to Discipline with Young Children*. Telshare Publishing Company, Inc. Chelsea, MA. 1982.

CHAPTER 15

The Partnership with Parents

Child care and early education is a partnership with parents. While working with parents can be a challenge, many child care professionals list this part of the job as one of the most enjoyable aspects of their work . . . right up there with the joys of watching children grow and develop. Supporting families can be tremendously rewarding. It makes you conscious of the real contribution you are making to society.

Most teachers of very young children are naturally empathetic to the initial fear, confusion and grief of children who are being left in child care for the first time. We "feel for them" and try to make it better by cuddling them and trying to comfort them. Sometimes, however, child care staff fail to have empathy with the distress of *parents* during this adjustment period. It is possible, if one has seen many children and parents make successful adjustments, to become impatient with those who seem to be taking too long. Remember that we are fighting instinct here, so try hard to be tolerant.

HELPING PARENTS ADJUST

For parents to trust you, they must have confidence that you know what you are doing, and that you care about their child. Time spent getting to know them and earning their trust will pay off in smoother relationships.

A "Get Acquainted" Interview with the Child's Primary Caregiver

It is important for parents to meet with the child's primary caregiver ahead of time for a "get-acquainted interview." It gives you a chance to get to know each other. This will make it much easier to talk in the weeks to come as the child and parent make their adjustments.

Take the time to explain all aspects of your program. Tell the parents what they will need to bring and where to put the child's things in your room. Also discuss how you will communicate with them—notes, phone calls, conferences, etc. Make sure the parent knows how to sign the child in and out, and find out who will be picking the child up and when. If someone other than the child's regular caregiver will be receiving the child in the mornings (if the child arrives before the caregiver's regular hours), introduce the parent to that person.

Also during this get-acquainted interview do some careful listening. Invite the parents to tell you as much as they can about their child. What does he enjoy doing most at home? What are his eating preferences and sleeping patterns? Be sure to find out about any special health considerations—allergies, etc. At this time, talk specifically about separation issues with children. Discuss what you will both do and what to expect.

Parent and Child Visits Prior to Enrolling

Strongly encourage the parent to visit the program together with the child for at least one morning before actually starting in the program. It is ideal if parents can stay until the child feels comfortable. Given this opportunity, toddlers often feel free to explore the new environment and join in on activities, simply going back to "touch base" with the parent every once in a while. The parent can separate gradually, staying shorter and shorter amounts of time from day to day.

There is another important advantage to such visits. The *parent* will have a much clearer image of what goes on during the day, the routine, the other children, and how you handle situations, and in the process is gaining trust in you as a caregiver.

Talk to Parents About the Child's Adjustment

It helps tremendously to call the parent during the day to let her know how the child is doing. Also tell parents, it's okay to call the center at any time. Some may fear such a call is intrusive, or indicates they are mistrustful. Make them feel comfortable about calling.

Share the good news. Be sure to tell parents if their child particularly enjoyed an activity, played well with other children, or seemed to enjoy large parts of the day. Hearing the little details makes a big difference. An instant photo would be nice.

Congratulate both the parent and the child when there is obvious progress. "Timothy is really gaining confidence. He comes right in now and is quickly involved with the other children. We all need to give ourselves a pat on the back!"

Understand Parents' Ambivalent Feelings

Sometimes caregivers feel like they can't win. The parent feels bad when the child cries and is having a hard time adjusting. On the other hand, as soon as the child makes an easy transition into the program and goes to the caregiver eagerly, parents also feel bad. "I'm losing my baby." Some parents learn to accept this happily, realizing their child is growing and her world is expanding. Some parents, however can't hide the touch of jealousy they have for the caregiver. They may come right out and tell you they are jealous—a very healthy response. Some parents may become overly critical or "picky" as a way of telling themselves that nobody can take as good care of their child as they can. In either case, it takes some extra understanding and support from you.

Reassure them that parents are always number one in the child's mind and they can never be replaced. Make an effort to point out how their child responds to them:

"Did you see how his face lit up when you came into the room? He had a good time today, but his face only looked like that when you came in. You are certainly number one for this little guy!"

"Look at that hug! Mommy certainly is number one around here!"

It's even harder on the parent when the child clings to you at the end of the day and doesn't want to go home, or calls you "Mommy." Reassure parents that many children this age simply have trouble making transitions of any type. Often the same child who cries in the morning separating from the parent will cry again in the afternoon separating from the caregiver. Give the child an affectionate hug and say, "I know . . . it is hard to say good-bye to people sometimes. But now it is time to go home and have dinner and have fun there. See you tomorrow!"

When the child calls you "Mommy," it does not mean that she no longer knows who her parent is. Children just acquiring language often "generalize" meanings. To a young child, "Mommy" may mean any adult female in a nurturing role. Make light of this mistake. "Hey . . . I'm not your mommy. I'm your 'Miss Jeanie.' I love you and I take care of you some of the time . . . but you only have one mommy and she is very special."

Most of all, treat parents with patience, kindness, and empathy. Let them know that you understand how difficult this is for them.

HELPING THE CHILD ADJUST

Toddlers and two-year-olds differ greatly in their ability to adjust to child care. Some children will enter eagerly, intrigued by all the toys and delighted to have children to play with. Their worry about being separated from their parents will be noticable only in subtle ways. Sometimes children who seem to be adjusting well will burst into tears as soon as their parents arrive. It's as though they have been working hard to control their feelings all day, and now they know it is safe to let them out. Other children will enter warily and spend most of their time just watching other children, taking only very cautious steps of involvement with encouragement from you. Some children will cling to you and cry for long periods of time. All of these children need special attention from you.

The first thing that must happen is that the child must feel safe. He needs to know that you are his protector—that you won't let other children hurt him. You become his "safe place." New children may spend a lot of time hanging onto your leg. (That's why toddler teachers walk funny!) Even if a child is relatively non-verbal, it helps to say, "I am here to take good care of you and play with you while your mommy (or daddy) is away."

Help the child move out from your side. Once the child seems relatively comfortable and at ease, try to engage her in some one-on-one play. Play dough, peek-a-boo, rolling a ball or truck back and forth, digging in the sand box, are all possibilities. Other children are likely to be attracted to the activity, giving the child pleasant social associations. When she sees you as a play partner adjustment may come faster.

Home Visits

Home visits are time-consuming and sometimes anxiety-producing for caregivers and parents alike, but with proper preparation, they can be fun and pleasant and go a long way to helping a child make a good adjustment to your program. The parents must know that you are not visiting the home to evaluate them, but simply to get to know them and their child better. When you show up at a child's home, he sees you in a whole new light. You are less threatening in familiar surroundings. If you sit at the kitchen table and have a cup of tea with his mommy, the child (and the parent) will be more likely to see you as a friend. Focus on the child while you are there. Ask him to show you where he sleeps. Play with his toys with him. Enjoy being on "his turf."

Then when you see him back at the child care program you

can say, "Remember . . . I came over to play with you at your
house yesterday. Now you are here to play with me." During
the day, you can talk to the child about his home. "You sure
have a pretty kitty!" "I remember when we were in your room
together and played with your toys. We had fun."

Even if you cannot visit all the children at home, home visits
are especially helpful for the children who have the most trouble
adjusting to your program. Worth a try!

Security Toys

Many toddlers and two-year-olds have some "security toy" or
transitional object that they carry around with them and depend
on in times of stress. It might be a blanket, a stuffed animal, or
some other object. By all means, allow children to have these
with them in their child care setting. These objects can be very
helpful to the child trying to anchor himself in a strange, stressful
or new situation. These objects will eventually be put aside as
the child gets busy.

Pictures of Family

Ask parents to bring pictures of themselves and perhaps other
family members for the child to have at school. These could be
put behind a plastic frame and hung low where a child can go
over and touch them frequently. Or, consider encasing the photo
in clear plastic for the child to carry around with him. This tells
him that his parent has not forgotten him and will come back for
him.

A Picture of You to Go Home

Have someone take a picture of your face with a big, friendly
smile on it. (Use a non-instant camera which produces negatives
from film.) Have copies made so that each child in your program
can take one home. Encourage the parent to put up this picture
at home where the child can see it—low on the refrigerator, or
near the child's bed, perhaps. As parents tuck their child in at
night, they can say, "Mommy loves you, and Daddy loves you,
and Granny loves you and Miss Jeanie loves you . . ." This helps
make you a part of the child's "extended family."

Separation Rituals

It can help the child gain a sense of control over a situation if the parent and the child develop a certain ritual of actions that are repeated each time the child is dropped off at the child care program. It might include a bear hug, a nose to nose rub, a formal handshake, and waving good-bye out the window. This type of ritual helps some children feel that "all is right in the world."

COMMUNICATING WITH BUSY PARENTS

Staying in touch with parents on a daily basis is important for everybody's peace of mind. It builds trust between the parent and the caregiver. However, it may not always be possible to see parents and talk to them personally each day if parents and child care staff work different hours.

A Parent Information Center—An Introduction to Your Classroom

It's a nice idea to have a bulletin board close to the entrance of your room where you introduce yourself and your program to parents. It can be a place to share news items, request their help in saving materials, etc. Keep it attractive, organized and interesting. If you change things on it at least weekly it will help motivate parents to check it for information. Here are some items that might be on it:

- A picture and short note from each staff person. The note might describe her professional background, why she chose to work with young children, and a few personal facts to help parents know her or him better as an individual.
- A menu for the week.
- A copy of a typical daily schedule—when you eat, go outside, nap, etc.
- Activity plans—any special projects you plan to do that week. Include brief descriptions of the learning value of the planned activities.
- A brief note about what you did that day describing any special happenings as well as how the planned activity was received by the children.
- Snapshots of children and activities. (Instant cameras are espe-

cially helpful.) Be sure to add descriptive captions. A photo album could be close by with collections of past activities. Organize the photos according to curriculum/learning areas for added parent awareness.

- Cartoons, poems, etc. that are appropriate to your program.
- A clothing marker pen for adding names to unmarked children's clothing.

Parent Message Center

Create a system for leaving notes and messages that affords more privacy than a bulletin board. This is where you might put notes about how the child's day went and what he did, diapering/toilet training progress, what the child ate, tuition receipts, etc. Likewise, parents should have a way to leave you messages. Many attractive variations of the systems described below have been devised.

- You could sew a "pocket" board, with one large pocket for each child in your program. A label could be stuck on each pocket.
- Coffee cans can be covered with attractive self-adhesive paper and taped together on their side in a pyramid formation to provide "mailboxes" for each family.
- Shoebags are sometimes used effectively.

PARENT CONFERENCES

Even though you make an effort to talk to parents frequently and communicate with them well in writing, it is important to schedule regular parent conferences where you can sit down and talk about their child's progress and any feedback they have about the program. Good child care programs are growing places for all people involved, children, staff, and parents. Well done parent conferences combined with good, on-going, informal communications benefit everybody.

Schedule an early conference just a few weeks after the child has enrolled. This is when parents have the most questions and need the most reassurance. Then schedule conferences on a regular basis thereafter. Most programs have formal parent conferences two times a year and "as needed" problem-solving sessions in between.

It's interesting that both parents and caregivers can approach conferences with anxiety. While caregivers may fear that parents will be critical of the job they are doing, parents sometimes think that their parenting skills are constantly being judged by the caregiver. It helps to look at parent conferences as an opportunity to make new friends. Being well-prepared ahead of time will lessen the anxiety. It helps to role-play a conference ahead of time in a staff meeting, anticipating difficult questions and your responses. A hint: schedule the friendliest parents first, to build confidence.

What Do You Cover in a Conference?

- Parents like to know what goes on during the day. Your class photo scrapbook can be an easy starting point. You can also take the opportunity to talk about what children are learning in typical activities.
- You also need to be specific. Parents like to hear about what their child particularly enjoys. What seem to be his favorite activities? Does he have any special friends? Show some samples you have saved of the child's work, or a description of a play episode.
- Share the anecdotal records you have been keeping about the child. What progress do you see the child making in various aspects of development—language, social, emotional, motor skills, etc.
- Bring up any concerns you have. Ask the parents for their insights. (It is advisable to discuss any concerns with your director first.) See if the parents can shed any new light on the situation. Ask for their advice or cooperation in coming up with a "plan of attack" on the problem. When you've decided what to try, you might also decide to get together again at a later date to evaluate the results.
- Invite the parents to bring up any problems or concerns they would like to talk about. Some parents may be reluctant to voice any concerns (others will have no trouble!), so be sure to ask.
- Start and end the conference on a positive note. Focus on what

the child is doing well. Thank the parents for coming and express your desire to continue to work closely. Most important, convey the feeling that you like their child and value the child's uniqueness.

RESPECTING AND REFLECTING CULTURES OF FAMILIES IN YOUR PROGRAM

We live in a diverse and changing society with people of many different backgrounds. It may take some sensitivity working with parents whose background is very different from your own, but it's well worth it. You will find that families from different cultures can add great richness to your program.

If the parents do not speak English, make an effort to find an interpreter so you can talk to them about their child. These parents have the same feelings and anxieties about child care as all other parents—often magnified by their strange surroundings—so give them this consideration. Always remember the magic of a smile that communicates across all language barriers.

You have a wonderful opportunity for building a multi-cultural program in your class, with the participation of parents. Ask *all* parents how they would like to contribute to your program. Some ideas:

- Perhaps they would like to do a simple cooking project with the children, or bring in a special food treat from their culture.
- Children would also enjoy hearing children's songs of a different culture. The child and the parent could perform together. It's also fun to hear familiar songs sung in a different language. "Happy Birthday" is a song sung in most languages, and they also probably have their own traditional birthday song that might become one of your class traditions as well.
- If a parent is proficient in English, perhaps he could tell one of their traditional folk tales in English or if he has a children's book from their country, he could show children the pictures and tell the story.
- Your housekeeping corner could contain samples of clothing worn in different cultures. Is there something that parents could bring and show them, or even leave in your housekeeping corner?

Also ask for empty food containers of foods of their culture to put in your housekeeping corner.

- Ask parents of all children to bring in pictures of their families, family celebrations, vacations, etc. as well as pictures of their homeland, if possible. It gives the new child some comfort in a strange situation, as well as sharing the culture. Do this with all of your children.

- Most of all, make all parents feel valued and welcome in your program.

RESOURCES

Galinsky, Ellen, *The Preschool Years*. Times Books. 1988.
This is an important and comprehensive book that guides parents in issues of child development, discipline, family life, work life and making all the pieces fit.

Galinsky, Ellen, *The Six Stages of Parenthood*, Addison Wesley, 1987.
This book shows how parents develop and change in their roles as their children develop. It is equally interesting for child care staff to give them insights into the parents they serve.

CHAPTER 16

A Safe Place for Toddlers

Safety in a setting with toddlers boils down to two main things: the built-in safety of the equipment and the facility, and the quality of adult supervision. Both are equally important.

The nature of toddlers makes safety a special concern. Toddlers have virtually no impulse control. In this "into everything" stage, they go to whatever is in front of their eyes without calculating any potential danger. They are not good at predicting cause and effect, like what a swing will do on its return trip. Toddlers are top-heavy and not well-coordinated, often stumbling or falling, so corners should be rounded, and surfaces softened. Toddlers are compulsive climbers and often climb on things that are not meant for that purpose and which may be unstable and dangerous. Stabilize any furniture used as room dividers by bolting pieces to the floor or to the wall, or to other pieces of furniture in an **L** or **X** formation. Add to all of this the fact that everything is likely to go into their mouths at one time or another, so adults must guard against potential choking and poisoning. Toys which have small pieces that are appropriate for older children may pose a hazard for toddlers. All staff should be trained in CPR for children as well as basic first aid.

Behavior control is another safety concern. Adults must be alert to protecting toddlers from each other and teach them appropriate ways to get their needs met without hurting each other. Make sure all staff with responsibility for supervising children, including volunteers, have specific training and know which behaviors to allow, and when and how to intervene, set limits and redirect children into more acceptable activities.

This safety checklist that follows presents some basic safety issues to be aware of, but don't limit yourself to these. Rewrite the safety checklist and add to it so that it is appropriate for your particular environment. Make plans to *use* your safety checklist on a regular basis, at least once a month.

Any person working with toddlers must learn to be constantly alert for any possibly hazardous situation. Children at this age must never be unsupervised, even for a moment. Most important, stay *vigilant*. Watch children closely and don't get distracted talking to other adults or allow your mind to wander. Safety is an *attitude*.

SAFETY CHECKLIST

SAFETY WITH TOYS AND EQUIPMENT

- Toys are in good repair and there are no sharp edges.
- Sharp objects like adult scissors and knives are kept out of reach of children.
- Furniture at child-height is free of sharp edges.
- Wooden furniture and toys are free of splinters.
- Cords from blinds or draperies are tied high and out of reach of children.
- Safety plugs are in all electrical outlets.
- Any appliance cords are out of reach of children.

SAFETY OF DOORS

- Signs are on the outside of doors warning people to open slowly and carefully, in case a child is behind them.

- To prevent fingers being pinched in doors children are discouraged from playing near them. Adults are careful when opening and closing doors.

SAFETY FROM FALLS

- Carpet and loose rugs are taped or tacked down for non-slip, non-trip stability.
- Furniture has maximum stability.

SAFETY FROM CHOKING

- The environment is free of small objects children can choke on (including toys designed for older children).
- There are no small, sharp objects on the floor or within reach of children that could cause damage if swallowed: safety pins, staples, thumb tacks, paper clips, hair pins, chipped paint, nails, etc.

SAFETY FROM POISONING

- All art materials offered to children are non-toxic.
- Adults' purses are stored out of sight, inaccessible to children.
- All medicines, including adult aspirin and pills, are stored in a place totally inaccessible to children.
- All medicines are kept in the original containers, with child-proof tops.
- All cleaning materials and poisonous substances are stored in a locked cabinet, kept in original containers and have child proof tops.
- Cages of any classroom pets are clean and the area around them is free of debris.
- Any plants in the room are non-poisonous.
- Safety latches are on low cabinet doors and drawers.
- Diaper pails are covered, and in a place inaccessible to children.
- Only lead free paint is used on walls and furniture.
- The poison control number is posted at all telephones.

SAFETY FROM HOT WATER

- Water temperature from hot water faucets is not warmer than 110 degrees.
- Adults do not drink coffee or hot beverages around children.

SAFE SUPERVISION

- State-required adult/child ratios are maintained at all times, inside and outside.
- A child is never left out of adult reach on a changing table, even for a moment.
- When the group is outside, children are not allowed to go inside alone to use the bathroom when there is no adult inside to supervise.
- Adults set appropriate limits on children's behavior, not allowing aggressive behaviors that physically endanger other children.
- Adults supervise swings, climbers and any other more dangerous pieces of equipment closely.

SAFETY OUTSIDE

- There are no gaps in the fence and gates. The fence is at least five feet high and reaches all the way to the ground. Gate latches work well and are out of the reach of children.
- Any spaces in climbers and other equipment are less than 4 inches or more than 8 inches so children will not get their heads stuck.
- There are adequate soft, shock absorbing surfaces under and extending beyond the sides of climbers, swings and slides.
- When sand is used as a cushioning surface, it is maintained at a depth of 8–12 inches.
- Swings have soft, "sling-type" seats.
- Swing supports are well anchored in concrete, so that the whole structure is stable. The concrete footings are buried so that children do not trip over them.
- Swings are well out of the traffic pattern so children do not routinely walk or ride in front of them.
- Slides are wide and low with sides on them to keep the child from slipping off.
- Adults routinely check the temperature of the slide before allowing children on it. If necessary, the slide is cooled down with water.
- Any wooden equipment, including the fence, is sanded and free of splinters.
- All bolts in equipment are recessed or smoothly rounded to

prevent gouges. There are no sharp edges where children could be cut.

- The yard is free of debris that children could choke on.
- There are no poisonous substances such as poisonous berries, mushrooms, animal feces or poisonous plants.
- There are no electrical hazards such as electrical wires, exposed air conditioners, or fuse boxes that children could reach from climbing structures or anywhere else.

REDUCING THE RISK OF KIDNAPPING

A combination of good written records and procedures, thorough staff training, and specific communication with parents can significantly reduce the risk of the nightmare of kidnapping becoming a reality in your program.

- Have a daily sign-in/sign-out sheet for all children in the program. It should have a space for the name of the child, the date, the time in, the time out, and the name of the person picking the child up.
- Know the parents of each child in your group. If their work hours don't coincide with yours, arrange a special meeting to get acquainted and keep in touch on a regular basis.
- Maintain detailed records of all children in your care, even "drop-ins" or children who are trying you out on a temporary basis. On the child's enrollment form, have the parent list any other adults who may pick up the child.
- Put a picture of each child in his or her file.
- In your enrollment interview, ask parents if there is any situation you should be aware of, such as a custody battle.
- Stress to parents the importance of letting you know of any changes in who will be picking the child up on a given day, if it is someone not listed on the enrollment form. This should be in writing, in case the person who is told in the morning is not there when the child is picked up in the afternoon.
- All staff members including cooks, bus drivers and substitutes, should know they may never release a child to someone they don't recognize. New staff are the people most likely to release a child to an unfamiliar adult. They should ask for *picture* ID such as a driver's license, and then check the name with those

listed on the child's enrollment form or emergency card. Even though grandparents, and others, may be annoyed at first, they usually appreciate the extra caution when they understand it is for the child's safety.

- If a parent calls to notify you of an emergency pick up by someone not on the child's form, verify that it is really the parent who is calling you. One good method is to call back at the parent's work number and ask, "Did you just call me?"

- Have an "emergency card" for each child to keep accessible in the classroom. It should duplicate information on the child's enrollment form, including phone numbers where parents can be reached, who can and cannot pick up the child, and the names of people to contact if the parent cannot be reached. It should also contain an emergency medical release.

- Be especially cautious if you need to evacuate the building for any reason—fire drills, bomb threats, etc. Take your sign-in sheets and emergency cards with you and check children off by name.

- Field trips require special precautions. Take a list of the children on the trip and their emergency cards along and make frequent head counts. Have extra adults to ensure that children are well supervised. Bathrooms can be a problem. Bring children all into the ladies room, as a group.

- Make sure all children are well supervised at all times, especially on the playground.

- Don't allow people not connected to your program, or hired to do so, to take pictures of the children.

- Beware of strangers, even in the guise of prospective parents. Have someone monitor the entrance of your building (if you are working in a child care center), keeping track of who is coming and going. Don't let people walk through the center to look around, *unaccompanied by a staff person*, even if they say they are thinking of enrolling their child.

- Don't let strangers in to use phone. If it is an emergency, make a call for them. Don't leave people alone in the office—they could go through children's files, take money, etc.

- Do not give information over the phone about whether or not a child is enrolled or in attendance that day.

- If you are faced with a situation where an unauthorized person persists in trying to take a child, be firm and direct. Do not inform the person where the child is. If she already knows and you are unable to keep the child from her, tell her in a firm voice that you will call the police immediately. Try to talk the person out of it.

- If someone succeeds in illegally taking a child, try to get a description of the car and the license plate number. Call the police immediately. Then notify the parent or legal guardian and call your state child care licensing office immediately to report the incident. Make a written report, recording all details as accurately as possible.

It is unfortunate that child care providers must take such extreme precautions, but the children's safety is your most important responsibility.

RESOURCES

Kendrick, Abby Shapiro, Roxanne Kaufmann and Katherine P. Messenger, editors, *Healthy Young Children, A Manual for Programs*. NAEYC, Washington, DC, 1988.
This valuable resource has a thorough section on safety in the child care environment including a complete listing of poisonous plants, and resources and organizations to write to for further information.

CHAPTER 17

Staying Alive
as a Professional

I would like to use these last pages to speak to the reader in a very personal way. In my 20 years in the early childhood profession, I have seen many fine individuals come and go . . . unfortunately, more going than coming. Our field is facing a major crisis—there are not enough good people choosing this work. I want good people to choose this field and to stay in this field . . . to give it a real commitment. Likewise, I would like our society to give a real commitment to children and the early childhood professionals who serve children and families. So I am giving you some words of advice about staying alive and growing as an early childhood professional.

GET THE PIECE OF PAPER. Even though you may know a great deal about children, it is important to have some outside authority acknowledge that. People who are looking for care for their children, and people who will want to hire you need some "benchmark," some assurance that you have a basic level of competence. So, do get your CDA or AA degree or BS degree in early childhood education. One probable benefit—you will be more sure that you are doing the right things with children, and you will know *why* you are doing these things. You will also have an added measure of professional pride.

KEEP LEARNING. A good professional never "closes the book" on her or his own personal growth. There is always more to know, something new to find out about. Learning doesn't stop when you finish a class or earn a Child Development Associate credential, or get a degree in early childhood education. Perhaps the most exciting phase of professional development is what I call the "now what" phase. That is when you as an individual, motivated only by your own interest, decide what you will explore next.

DEVELOP AND USE CRITICAL JUDGMENT.   You need to know how to "sift." There is a lot of material being marketed to early childhood professionals, much of it excellent, some of it not so terrific. Become a critic. Learn not to trust something just because it is in print or someone has manufactured it. Measure everything against what you know about children. Learn to trust your own judgment.

BECOME PART OF THE NETWORK.   Join a professional organization. You need to mingle with other thinking, intelligent people who have chosen the same line of work you have. It's important to meet periodically, not only to learn new things, but to be "reconfirmed." You will be reminded of good practices, reinforced to go back and do what you know is right, and you will be able to talk about what you do with greater conviction. There are a number of good organizations to join. Two good starting points are The National Association for the Education of Young Children (phone: 800-424-2460) and the National Association for Family Child Care (phone: 800-359-3817). Call their numbers to find out how to connect with your local chapter.

TEACH OTHER ADULTS.   The saying goes that the best way to learn something is to teach it. There is really some truth to this. Presenting a workshop or a parent meeting on a topic can sharpen your knowledge. You have to consider, what is important to know about this topic? What does someone need to know first before they can understand other concepts? Whether you have 45 minutes to do a workshop at a staff meeting or you teach a class that stretches over a whole semester, you never have enough time to cover everything of possible interest pertaining to the topic. How do you inspire participants to go on learning independently?

EVALUATE YOURSELF.   Just how good are you? Where can you be better? How can you go about improving your skills? These are questions you need to ask yourself continuously. As a starting point, you need to know how your employer is evaluating you. If you don't already have it, ask your employer for a copy of the criteria by which you will be evaluated. Family child care providers who work for themselves can call the National Association of Family Day Care, 800-359-3817 for some good self-evaluation materials. Now, go beyond the list your employer will use. Add your own criteria (just for your own use). List the things that are important to you personally.

EVALUATE YOUR PROGRAM. Every early childhood program should have some system in place to formally evaluate the quality of the service to children on a regular basis, at least twice a year. It's easy to become complacent, so it is useful to take a step back and analyze what you are doing, always asking if you can be doing something better. Ask a trusted early childhood professional friend not involved with your operation to come and look at your program with fresh eyes. There are several very useful tools on the market to help you with this process. Be sure to add your own items to the lists.

The INFANT/TODDLER ENVIRONMENT RATING SCALE by Thelma Harmes, Richard Clifford and Debby Cryer gives you a very useful framework to start from in giving your program a long, critical look. DEVELOPMENTALLY APPROPRIATE PRACTICE IN EARLY CHILDHOOD PROGRAMS SERVING CHILDREN FROM BIRTH THROUGH AGE 8, Sue Bredekamp, Editor, published by NAEYC, serves as a good measuring stick.

CONSIDER ACCREDITATION. Working toward accreditation by the National Academy of Early Childhood Programs, (a division of NAEYC) is one excellent way an entire child care staff can work together in a systematic manner to improve the quality of their service. The National Association for Family Day Care has also developed an accreditation program for family child care homes. The major goal of both of these accreditation programs is to improve the quality of care provided to children in this country. No matter how good you are to start out with, there is always room for improvement. Another major advantage to these programs is the great sense of professional pride participants feel.

BECOME AN EVANGELIST. There are many ways to be an advocate for young children. At this moment in our history, we desperately need people to speak out about the importance of quality early childhood programs. There is much to be done! Your voice and experience are needed! An excellent resource book with many helpful ideas is: SPEAKING OUT: EARLY CHILDHOOD ADVOCACY, by Joan Lombardi and Stacie G. Goffin, published by NAEYC.

PRACTICE GOOD ETHICS.   Ethics is a big topic that touches on many issues of your work. One major area of ethics is that of confidentiality. You will have access to private information about the families you serve, including their income or employment status, relationships, pregnancies, family traumas, and custody issues. Never talk about any child's problems or family situations to other parents or staff who are not directly involved with the child. Keep private information private.

Another important issue of ethics is awareness of child abuse. All staff working with children should have specific training on how to recognize possible abuse and what to do about it. You are required by law to report any suspected child abuse. Talk to your director immediately if you suspect anything. Another unfortunate issue is the possibility of child abuse by child care staff. Talk to your director anytime you have uneasy feelings about the conduct of another staff person. This is always a difficult and uncomfortable issue, because you do not want to "rat" on a fellow employee, but remember, the welfare of the child must come first. If your center has not had specific training on these topics recently, see if you can arrange it. Local communities usually have many resources to call on.

PRESENT A PROFESSIONAL APPEARANCE.   This does not mean that you should show up for work in a suit and heels—in fact, that would be highly inappropriate! People who work with toddlers and twos need to be comfortable on the floor, stable on their feet and able to move quickly. Pants and flat shoes work best. Clothing should be washable so that you are not forever shying away from messes, which are inevitable. Professional dress means a neat, clean appearance. Leave your bangley, dangley jewelry at home. Long nails can be a hindrance. You don't want your clothes to get in your way, but you do want to be taken seriously by other adults. So, look as nice as possible every day, and when you are addressing a parent meeting, attending a conference or speaking to your legislature, dress up.

Your most important accessory is your smile. Sometimes the

ultimate challenge of a professional is to put personal problems and stress aside and be pleasant to children, parents and other staff. Train yourself to smile and allow minor irritations to roll off your back.

BE A TEAM PLAYER.   Your relationship with your coworkers can make all the difference in enjoying your work. Child care is difficult, stressful work. When adults pull together and support each other, the job becomes easier. It is everything from arriving at work 5 minutes early or volunteering to help with a task, to giving helpful advice and ideas to a new employee, to providing a listening ear, and help in problem solving. When I interviewed child care workers who had been working in the same place many years, *all* of them mentioned their affection and respect for their co-workers as one of the primary reasons for sticking around. Good staff relations are well worth nurturing!

LOOK FOR "GIGGLES AND GOOSEBUMPS."   My friend, Dr. Grace Mitchell, used to require all staff members at their monthly staff meetings to report on one "giggle," (funny thing that happened) or "goosebump" (an incident that reminds you of why you chose this field) that had happened to them in their work in the past month. This starts the staff meeting on a positive note. More important though, knowing this is an expectation, it makes people look for positive things that happen on a daily basis. Is it the first hug you receive from a reluctant toddler? Is it the parent who expresses sincere appreciation? Is it watching a toddler imitate your gestures and mannerisms? Maybe it's the funny way a child expresses herself. This technique will keep you focusing on the positive aspects of your work—the fun stuff.

STICK AROUND.   The crisis of staff turnover in the field of early childhood education has been well-publicized. It presents major recruiting and training challenges to organizations providing care. The most serious consequence of high staff turnover, though, is the emotional damage to children. The little ones don't see you as employee doing a job. They see you as an important adult in their lives—someone they trust—someone who loves them. When a beloved caregiver leaves, the children feel rejected and abandoned.

Focus on the big picture . . . the very real difference you are making in the quality of life for small children and their families, and how this ultimately benefits society. As an individual, you have the power to make your program a better service to children. You have the power to make the field of earlier childhood education stronger. You have the power to make the lives you touch a little bit better.

Organizations:

National Association for the Education of Young Children (NAEYC) 1834 Connecticut Avenue, N.W., Washington, DC 20009-5786. Toll free phone number: 800-424-2460.

National Association for Family Day Care (NAFDC), 725 15th St. NW, Suite 505, Washington, D.C. 20005. 800-359-3817.